Vacancy In the (Relationship) Rabbit Hole

How to Escape Toxic Love, Re-Define Self Worth and Beat Every Narcissist at The Game of Life

Zari Ballard
(NAR Coach)

TheNarcissisticPersonality.com

Copyright © 2021 Zari Ballard

All Rights Reserved.

ISBN: 9798704864882
Independently published

OTHER BOOKS BY ZARI BALLARD

When Love is a Lie
Narcissistic Partners & the Pathological Relationship Agenda

Stop Spinning, Start Breathing
A Codependency Workbook for Narcissist Abuse Recovery

When Evil Is a Pretty Face
Narcissistic Females & the Pathological Relationship Agenda

All of the above books are available in digital and paperback versions and can be purchased from Amazon, Kindle, Barnes & Nobles, iTunes, and other online resellers. This book and *When Love Is a Lie* are also available on Audible

TABLE OF CONTENTS

Note to Readers:	*Change Your Perspective*	
Introduction:	*The Relationship Rabbit Hole*	1
Chapter I:	*Narcissists & The Game of Life*	7
Chapter II:	*Aliens Among Us*	15
Chapter III:	*Simplified Evil*	23
Chapter IV:	*The Break-Up*	29
Chapter V:	*Wanting to Believe*	35
Chapter VI:	*Signs of the End Times*	43
Chapter VII:	*Trauma Bonding*	51
Chapter VIII:	*Relationship Amnesia*	69
Chapter IX:	*Logical Self-Worth*	75
Chapter X:	*The No-Contact Rule*	81
Chapter XI:	*What's Your Intention?*	95
Chapter XII:	*Avoiding Triggers*	105
Chapter XIII:	*The Co-Parenting Dilemma*	119
Chapter XIV:	*Suffering Is a Process*	129
Chapter XV:	*The Truth About Forgiveness*	139
Chapter XVI:	*Vacancy In the Rabbit Hole*	153
	Final Thoughts	163
	Speak w/ Zari	166
	ABOUT THE AUTHOR	167

A Note to Readers:

Change Your Perspective, Change Your Life

Please know that, in this book, although I typically refer to the narcissistic partner as being of the male gender, it is only used as a general term and as a matter of convenience since I speak from personal experience. Narcissists come disguised as boyfriends, husbands, wives, girlfriends, mothers, fathers, sisters, brothers, sons, daughters, bosses, and co-workers. In the end, the suffering is all the same. Clearly, narcissists can be male or female and I try to refer to both genders as often as possible.

Secondly, because *Vacancy In the (Relationship) Rabbit Hole* and all content contained therein is based solely upon my personal experience and perspective, I *deliberately exclude* any type of clinical "information". In other words, I offer no medical or psychological explanation for narcissistic behavior because it really has no bearing on your recovery.

This book is about healing from the narcissistic nonsense and beating narcissists at their own game. It's about following the path that leads away from our self-induced suffering. In a relationship rabbit hole, we are distracted from our own happiness. I want to show you the way out. Often, in order to change our lives, it is a matter of simply changing our perspective about that which ails us. On the proper path, we then can see, with clarity, that self-worth should never be based on the bad behaviors of narcissists but rather on the authenticity and integrity we create for ourselves day to day as we play along in this Game of Life.

Thank you for reading…

Introduction:
The Relationship Rabbit Hole

There are people in this world who've lived their entire lives without ever going down the relationship rabbit hole. I wasn't one of those people. For me, life in this particular hole dragged on for thirteen years although I didn't officially understand the true nature of my emotional habitat until I was eight years in. It was at that eight year mark that I began to *really* question the bizarre behaviors of my partner...behaviors that I often dismissed as quirky (albeit, hurtful)...behaviors that caused me to behave in ways that were totally out of my fairly laid-back character. It was also at this point that I had my "a-ha" moment, putting together for the first time the puzzle pieces of my broken love story. This life-jarring moment was the culmination of an experience that only those who have lived it first-hand could ever understand.

I refer to this particular emotional realm of existence as a relationship rabbit hole because it is what it is...a dark, dreary tunnel filled with unexplainable turmoil and inexplicable emotion. When we love a toxic person such as a narcissist or sociopath, we spend much of our time in this rabbit hole and will become quite acclimated. Our eyes adjust to the darkness and our skin becomes just thick enough so that most bullshit rolls off. It is a hole that feels endless...and somewhere between its ominous opening and this infinite endlessness is where our toxic love resides. Reluctantly attached to this toxicity, we will venture into the darkness as far as we can go. It is a precarious time during which we will accept - and *settle* for - certain bad behaviors from our partner that we never would before. This acceptance and willingness to settle, of course, is how we get stuck in the rabbit hole, blinded by "love" and unable to feel our way out.

Now, there will be those times, periodically, when common sense comes to call. We will snap to attention, surfacing to the light to get on with our lives. We will do our best to leave the pain behind us. During this time, we actually feel free. We announce to the world that we would *never* go back. But toxicity creeps and is forever patient, one finger poised above the reset button. Narcissists, you see, because of their chameleon-like qualities, can live in the light quite comfortably. They have learned to blend in with the crowd. The rabbit hole, in fact, is a narcissist's *second* home and the one he reserves for us when the time is right and the reset engages. In the light, the narcissist appears to be normal and he or she knows it. *I'm sorry, baby, I don't even remember what happened. All I know is I miss you*, came the whisper from my rabbit hole. The tug is familiar but we pretend we're feeling it for the first time. Suddenly, the toxicity that we hate intoxicates us *in a good way,* like a bouquet of fucking flowers. This is insanity at its best. We begin to wobble, drunk on the madness of it all, and the suffering restarts. Silent treatments, gas-lighting, triangulation, and other narcissistic niceties pick up right where it all left off. At this point, it is clear that common sense has long left the building.

The irony about life in the relationship rabbit hole is that, as we become accustomed to the abuse, the rabbit hole becomes the one place where we feel secure…the one place where we actually find a *reprieve* from the suffocating separation anxiety. Again, only someone who has *been there, done that* will understand what I mean by this. The rabbit hole becomes both *the last place and the only place* we care to reside because it's the one place to which the narcissist will always return. And the narcissist knows this because he or she has studied how we think. We will journey own the rabbit hole to find our narc and inevitably lose ourselves in the process. After all, it is the mere shadow of our former self that he or she so adores and it is only our mere shadow that can live in the rabbit hole.

It's time to put up the vacancy sign, my friends. The rabbit hole, by its very dark nature, will suck the light from our soul if we allow it. We venture down the tunnel for many reasons - out of love, curiosity, desperation, and to offer forgiveness or even beg for it. We are bound and determined to uncover clues to our mind-boggling mystery. This person we love is always a stranger and our endless search for evidence leads us to very muddy waters. One girl that I counseled would agonize over the lengths to which she would go to investigate the obvious. She often put herself in precarious positions, risking her self-respect and general reputation just to gather the evidence necessary for a confrontation that never takes place. Finally, as we all inevitably do, she had to stop and ask herself just how far down the rabbit hole she was willing to go.

Yes, the rabbit hole is the domicile of narcissists and sociopaths and the place where he or she feels the most comfortable. Since we love this person, we will selflessly pretend to be comfortable as well. We want to be where he or she is at all times and will adjust to the darkness of the tunnel while at the same time trying to shine the light of love within it. We spend a whole lot of time trying to figure it all out…why they do what they do and say what they say and why they never mean what they say or say what they mean. We agonize over a narc's willingness to cheat and how easily he or she will lie about it. We demand to know why they leave and how they can do it as if our history together meant nothing. We suffer through silent treatments and disappearances that make no sense. We will wait, often for months, for the inevitable hoover…the special invite…to come back to the rabbit hole. In our twisted reality, we actually believe that we belong there.

So, why do narcissists do what they do? To understand this, you've got to understand the game. My theory is that there really is just one all-encompassing incentive in the narcissist's relationship agenda…one all-important motivation for the nonsense that is securely connected to everything else. This motivation is key to his or her winning in their twisted version of the Game of Life...even if no one else on the game board is aware that they are playing. To understand and accept this simple theory is key to mentally breaking free from the madness. Allow me to explain...

Chapter I:
Narcissists & The Game of Life

Most of us remember a board game from our childhood called The Game of Life. This game, which is still in production today, is a family-inspired game that takes players on a journey from birth to death through a variety of situations including love, marriage, work, and so forth. The "winner" of the game, according to the rule booklet, is the player who, at the end, has accumulated more wealth and happiness than the other players. He or she will have done this presumably through hard work and doing the right thing.

Now, to understand how narcissists work and think in our modern world, I ask you to imagine a board game much like The Game of Life but with a slight variation on the methods of play. In this modern day version, the world is different than it was in our childhood. There are players at the table with narcissistic personalities that we neither recognize nor understand. We see these players as normal and, therefore, we are naïve to their intention…but, as I am here to tell you, intention in life is everything. To understand the natural mindset of narcissists, we have to analyze how they move through everyday situations…how they see the world and the ultimate goal at the finish line. Stay with me here and it will all start to make sense.

In this new, modern version of the Game of Life, players who have a narcissistic personality will always play by a different set of rules than everyone else on the game board. To all *normal* players, the point of The Game of Life, as reflected in the rule book, is not so much about winning as it is about collecting as many Happiness points as possible without bumping other players off the board. The narcissist, on the other hand, sees the finish line very differently. To him (or her), the point of the Game is *indeed all about* bumping players while still moving forward.... and *to hell* with the happiness points.

To ensure a fair start in Life, each player begins The Game with ten Conscience Cards. As players move along the board, they will have the option of exchanging Conscience Cards for Happiness points depending upon different scenarios presented. For example, if, by the roll of the dice, a normal player does happen to bump another player, it is usually done with regret and this player may choose, at that moment, to either forfeit the move or continue on ahead. If the choice made is dictated by Conscience (i.e. forfeiting the move), one card is exchanged for ten Happiness points. If the player has no regret about the bump, then he/she keeps his or her cards and continues on. This is how Happiness is collected and, ideally, the winner of The Game would be the one who finishes with the most points but the least number of cards, having chosen, in large part, to journey through Life doing the right thing. And while players can also choose to begin The Game as a single player or in relationship mode with another normal player, the aforementioned point of the game, for the most part, never changes.

A narcissistic player, on the other hand, will *always* play the Game in relationship mode while all the while secretly moving along the board determined to win completely on his own. To hide this evil intention, the narcissist often begins the game disguised as a "normal" player, whereby reducing, and possibly eliminating, the chance of his normal "player partner" from ever catching on, dropping out, or having him or herself booted from the game. The narcissist may even switch player partners mid-game without either partner knowing – a gaming strategy obviously intended to cause emotional distress and confusion and increase his overall chances of winning. For his normal player partner, these game behaviors definitely create a series of unique Life challenges. Finally, at games end, even with no Happiness points collected and all of his Conscience Cards in hand, a narcissist will, with total confidence, declare himself a winner despite the fact that he broke many hearts and almost every Life rule to get to the finish line.

Understand that the narcissist has but one true motivation in life and that is *to always be getting away with something*. Every day, that's all it's about! This is the secret to a narcissist's success. And in the narcissist's Game of Life, "getting away with something" isn't necessarily based upon a partner finding out or not finding out because this is just an *option* in the game. In fact, the narcissist *fully expects his or her partner(s)* to find out or, at the very least, to be suspicious because *then* he or she gets to practice the ability to deceive *after* the original deception. This is the next level up - the lie after the lie. First, the narcissist cheats and lies about it after which he or she is discovered and confronted and will gladly lie again. The narcissist practices the art of *never admitting to anything.* If the narcissist is exceptional and "polished", he or she may even compel the loving partner to apologize for HIS or HER bullshit behaviors and that's a BONUS in the game! This is what the narcissist's relationship agenda is all about …nothing more, nothing less.

Through clever and creative deception is how a narcissist hones his or her skills for any and all future targets. Everyone in the narcissist's life – you included – is practice fodder for his need to deceive and get away with it. And, as we know, deceiving can be about anything at all, even that which we'd consider to be the most trivial. This is why, as I've always said, a narcissist will lie even when the truth is a better story. If he went to one store, he'll say he went to another…because he can…because *he can get away with it and because we allow him or her to do it.* In the event that he *doesn't* get away with it…if he is caught in a lie red-handed and called out…well, he'll just try something else. He'll think up another lie. Practice makes perfect. This is where we become crazy, trying to understand why he or she keeps doing the same thing over and over. Truth and fiction within the relationship begins to blur. We begin to investigate, spy, stalk, and finagle - yet in the end we typically know less about the facts than we did at the start.

Because a narcissist admits to *nothing* unless his back is absolutely up against a wall (a rare occurrence), we become so confused and riddled with anxiety over day to day events that we end up saying nothing at all about anything. This, my friends, is part of the end game. In the narcissist's playbook, our obedient silence, our ability to look away, is a means to an end. Keeping a partner in a heightened state of anxiety is a desired result of the narcissist's nonsense. This is how he or she creates our reality and keeps us quiet. Our suffering not only turns the narcissist on mentally, it becomes the all-encompassing motivation *to lie bigger and better than before.* He or she will strive to get away with as much as possible with the least resistance in the shortest amount of time…and we reluctantly and inadvertently allow it to happen.

Look, when we're involved with people who play the Game of Life by a set of rules completely contrary to those rules that *we* hold sacred, we have to make decisions based on our conscience…on what we know to be true. Certainly we are not perfect, but, for the most part, our rules are based in morality. Choosing to play it safe, we can simply do "unto others" as we would have them do unto us. We attempt to treat others as we would like to be treated. Narcissists do not live this way. A narcissist knows right from wrong but simply doesn't care. We do NOT have to accept unacceptable and disrespectful behaviors from anyone. It takes no effort to be kind to the people who love you.

To get the most from this Game of Life, we have to be true to ourselves. *We must learn to live an authentic life.* While board games allow us the opportunity to play over and over, the *real* Game of Life awards us only one chance to get it right. Narcissists have no right imposing on our journey and we are not doomed to live in anyone's rabbit hole. The paths leading out of the tunnel are lighted and smooth if we open our eyes. I'm going to help you recognize these paths in a way that makes sense but I won't mince words. Sugarcoating the steps to recovery is a dangerous action and I don't believe you would want me to do this. I believe that you want it straight-up so that's how I'm going to do it.

The tips, tricks and ideas I share about eliminating toxic partners and creating a life of authenticity are my own but, believe me, they've been tried and tested. I've corresponded with and spoken to a large enough sample of good people over the last five years to know that these methods work. I discovered that recovery 1) works better as a team effort, and 2) should consist of LOGICAL alternatives to our twisted *victim* way of thinking. If a theory or thought process is logical, we will automatically remember it for future use. Logic is a comfortable fit that cannot be denied. Logic is simple and doesn't have to be explained to narcissists. Why? Because narcissists know "logic" all too well and they do not like it. You, however, will learn to love it once you know how to use it. You will win every time.

I'm not saying recovery from narcissist abuse syndrome is easy because it is not. There is no easy fix. But while the pain, unfortunately, is inevitable, the suffering – which is the *real* crippler - is completely OPTIONAL! Narcissistic nonsense is just that…NON-sense. It's actually so transparent that once we do "get it", our head and our heart automatically catch up. It's not rocket science, my friends.

Okay, so before we dig into some mind-tricks, let's talk a bit more about exactly what makes a narcissist so different from the "normal" population. Let's see what makes a narc tick, and why a life with this person is simply unsustainable.

Chapter II:
Aliens Among Us

As we know, at any given moment, there are literally millions of emotional vampires walking the planet disguised as human beings. We may label these vampires as narcissists, sociopaths, and psychopaths but, at the core, they are all the same but for varying degrees of evilness. These entities are not like us and therefore, we can't wrap our head around the behaviors. We will never know *exactly* how a narcissist *"feels and thinks",* thank God, because *we possess all the good qualities that a narcissist lacks.* However, to understand the dynamic, we don't *need* to know *exactly*…we just need to know *enough* and then call it. Accepting this small fact as truth will set us free but – alas - partners of narcs are notorious procrastinators. We hang in there, waiting on just one more piece of "evidence" when we've had more than enough to convict all along.

Those of us with experience know that there is something significant at the core that makes the narcissistic personality very different from our own. We understand that this difference is far bigger than the fact that this person is a "complete jerk" and we're not. We understand that having a narcissistic personality means that something at the core of this person's *very being* is missing and that this "lack of" provides some fairly evil capabilities. We also understand that there is no way for this person to simply obtain this missing ingredient or "get it back" and this is typically the biggest cause of our grief. A narcissist can't "get back" what a narcissist never had and, consequently, at the moment that we make this discovery, the relationship becomes a done deal. All efforts made after the fact to "fix" this person will always be futile. As a victim, it's akin to learning that our life partner who has an inoperable brain tumor simply doesn't care. While we sob, grieve, and search endlessly for cures, the narcissist casually moves along in the moment. Leave it to a narc to take Buddhist-based notions like mindfulness, detachment and living in the "moment" to a completely nefarious level.

So, what is it that someone who has a narcissistic personality lacks? What is this core human element that, without it, can transform a walking, breathing monster of emptiness into something even worse? And how does it happen? Is it possible that, for a narc, empathy simply never developed OR was never there to begin with? Perhaps, even worse, is it possible that a person with precursors to narcissism can, at some significant moment in time, *choose* not to feel certain things, whereby willfully allowing the "lack" to turn narcissistic? Is it a choice?

The missing ingredient, my friends, is *empathy*. Yup, good ole' empathy....the core element/quality/ingredient of human-to-human goodness that can be defined in a zillion different ways that all mean exactly the same thing. For example, below are just a handful of

definitions for empathy that I found online while doing some research for this book:

1. Identification with and understanding of another's situation, feelings, and motives.

2. the imaginative projection of a subjective state into an object so that the object appears to be infused with it

3. the ability to mutually experience the thoughts, emotions, and direct experience of others.

4. the capacity to recognize emotions that are being experienced by another sentient or fictional being

5. the power of understanding and imaginatively entering into another person's feelings

6. The ability to understand another person's circumstances, point of view, thoughts, and feelings

7. the ability to understand the thoughts, feelings or emotions of someone else.

8. the awareness of the thoughts, feelings, or states of mind of others, perhaps by means of some degree of vicarious experience of others' feelings or mental states.

9. the experience of understanding another person's condition from their perspective.

10. The ability of a person to place themselves in "another person's shoes", so to speak

Yes, empathy is what a "normal" person has (or feels) that narcissists, sociopaths, and psychopaths do not. In fact, it is this lack of empathy that is driving force behind all narcissistic behaviors. When a narcissist is part of a couple and the other person is "normal", it is this lack of empathy on the narc's part that will ultimately cause all of the suffering. The "normal" person, in fact, is referred to as an *empath* because they possess the qualities of compassion that narcissists do not. On certain websites/forums where sociopaths and narcissists gather to chat, the behaviors and "feelings" of *empaths* are openly mocked and demeaned. Yes, I've come to believe that the narcissist knows *exactly* what he or she is missing and is quite proud of it.

As I stated in **When Love Is a Lie**, a narcissist doesn't have to feel an emotion in order to understand how it works. In fact, the narcissist is an expert in how compassionate, normal people think and feel. To compensate for his or her empathetic lack, a narcissist cleverly learns to *pretend* and *impersonate,* mimicking the specific emotions needed to blend seamlessly into society. The female narc is especially good at this due to the natural nurturing tendencies of women. However, nothing lasts forever. The mask *will* fall as more and more people become aware of narcissism in relationships and what it all really means. Some emotions are easier to fake than others…and faking that one really understands and *feels* another person's pain is simply not that easy, even for a narcissist.

To be clear, 'empathy' is very different from *sympathy* and, in order to understand how seriously lacking a narc is in both, we have to make the distinction. If you remember one point from this book, remember this: *A narcissist can fake sympathy but he or she can never, ever fake empathy* and this is key to exposing a narcissist. The average narcissist *relies* on the fact that the average person has a less than average understanding of what separates empathy from sympathy. Normal people will always confuse the two and this is unfortunate. If we understood the distinction, we would recognize deception immediately and automatically know a person's true intention. Our **intuition**, by the way, *always* knows the difference between empathy (which can't be faked) and false signs of sympathy. This is why, despite a narcissist's talent for love-bombing, we can't shake the feeling that something is "off". While he or she is being "attentive" to our needs, we can't help but feel suspicious. This is our intuition saying, "Uh, that's no empathy FOOL! That's just a narc faking sympathy!"

Here's how I see it: When a person expresses empathy towards another person's situation, the feeling comes from that person's life *experience*. When we appreciate what another person is feeling because we've *been there*, walked in his or her shoes, or felt that exact same feeling at some point or at many points, we can do much more than sympathize with this person. For example, when my son was born, he was very ill and remained in the hospital NICU ward from birth until he was almost seven months old. It was a traumatic period of time that was always intensified by the fact that he could, at any moment, get unexpectedly sicker and die. During this time, I became close to the parents of other NICU babies and we empathized with each other in a capacity that is beyond words for me even now. To describe what myself and the other NICU parents felt toward each other's situation as sympathy doesn't even come close. Thirty years later, the thought still brings tears to my eyes because while 'sympathy' is good, 'empathy' is *bone deep* and can - and will - bring people from all walks of life together.

My thinking is that our ability to be empathetic is compounded and stored for future use every time we experience a situation, good or bad, that touches us on a personal level. Later on, when we happen across another person in that same or a similar situation, we instantly draw from our own experience and *feel* for that person. This is precisely why all of us who have experienced life with a narcissistic partner can relate to each other at the level that we do. Your story is my story is his story is her story. This is why our "a-ha" moment typically comes as we scour the internet, reading voraciously the stories of others who suffer from narcissistic abuse syndrome. This is why I can talk to complete strangers who call me for counsel as if I have known them all my life. They are me and I am them. Empathy is a connective tissue! This is also why those who have never had the experience of a narcissistic partner simply don't "get it" and probably never will. We can't blame people for this lack of understanding because the complexity and basic nature of this type of emotional abuse has to be experienced for a person to even fathom that it exists at all.

I've come to believe that as we get older, we automatically start to empathize more than we sympathize simply because our archive of meaningful experiences has grown bigger. To the contrary, a narcissist is completely incapable of feeling empathy because *he or she has no archive to draw from*. The events in a narcissist's life are momentary at best and YOU are simply an 'event' like any other. The narcissist has experienced many, many of the same situations we have, maybe even right alongside us, but the "takeaway" for a narc from these situations is completely different. We archive almost every experience in ways that enrich our ability to interact with people now and in the future. A narc, unfortunately, lives through all or most experiences *feeling nothing* and, therefore, this is exactly what he or she brings to the table when interacting with others – **nothing**. He or she simply can't 'relate'. The narc may *try* to relate (for a minute) but the interaction, in retrospect, is always awkward. A narcissist would rather fake it and flee rather than help to relieve the burden of another. A narcissist, no matter how busy in life, will always have an *empty archive* of experiences from which to draw from. For a narcissist, deception becomes the only solution. From our experience archive, as a "normal" player in the Game of Life, we identify quickly that *love is the answer* and then proceed to pay it forward. A narcissist would think that this is nothing more than the nonsense thinking of normal humans.

    My ex, for example, would disappear at the beginning of any crisis in my life - *no matter how small* – and only resurface when he felt enough time had passed for the situation to have resolved itself. For example, if I mentioned in passing that my car had broken down, he would typically disappear until I drove down to find him *in my car*, thus signaling that the crisis had obviously ended and his assistance was no longer needed. I find this memory humorous now but *still* completely unacceptable. I can't even count the letters and emails I've received from women whose narcissistic husbands never even made it to the births of their own children or who abandoned their families just shortly thereafter. Why would we even allow these things to occur? Because narcissist abuse syndrome is *real,* that's why.

The fact that a narcissist *can't feel* is reason enough to leave the relationship. It is the only evidence we really need if we would only accept it. Sure, we could, I suppose, muster up some *sympathy* for this person's inability to be human, but why do that? Why rack our brains trying to figure it out just to help this person and save the relationship? The simple truth is that a narcissist *can't* feel and this *isn't* a fixable problem. The narcissist doesn't care that he can't feel because he knows that simply faking an emotion will get the desired result. It's typically not until the narcissist's attempts at faking *empathy* fail miserably that we notice the slip of the mask. Then, and only then, do we seriously begin to wonder *what the hell is going on.* It is the narcissist's amazing ability to mess with our psyche that makes him or her appear to be so complicated. But to a narcissist, this manner of game play is not complicated at all. In fact, the mind-boggling dynamic I have described in this chapter is only complicated for the victim.

In my quest to pinpoint the narcissistic mind, I recently determined that the narc's agenda in all relationships can be boiled down to two simple intentions combined in a singular process. The truth is that narcissists are as simple as they are complicated and what they have learned to simplify is the 'evil' aspect of the pathology itself. This process, which involves, first, the intention to control and, second, the validation of that control, is key to how narc's operate in this Game of Life that we all play. So, let's talk about it that which is simple…

Chapter III:
Simplified Evil

One of the unique dynamics of a disordered personality is that from whatever angle we decide to examine it, the view *always* appears complicated. Of course, the narcissist will swear up and down that "complicated" is *far* too exaggerated a description and the problem, of course, is us, *right*? Consequently, when a narcissist scolds us for making mountains out of molehills, it's his or her attempt, as always, to make us doubt our intuition (better known as gas-lighting) and, for the most part, this tactic always works. Or does it?

In **When Love Is a Lie**, I describe an altercation with my ex where I was, for once, confidently laying out what I thought to be his methodical steps to sabotage the relationship. In a quick witted attempt to disarm me, he looked at me calmly and said, "Really, you're making me out to be far more complicated than I am. The truth is *I'm just a simple man.*" And it worked! Now, years later, I realize that he was telling the truth. I now refer to these moments of narcissistic truth-telling as *snippets of truth* and, believe me, back then, the moment was not lost on my narc. Finding his 'snippet' very clever in the moment, he then used *I'm just a simple man* as his new catch phrase for every argument where he felt he had to defend himself. It wasn't until much later, after receiving mail from readers describing similar circumstances, that I realized, by insisting that he was "just a simple man", my ex was – albeit inadvertently - providing me with the biggest clue *ever* into how these human anomalies really think.

What happens is this: because the antics of the narc are so mind-boggling, we, as the recipients, tend to trump them up, making the behaviors far more complicated than they really are. In the end, all this does is give the narcissist far more credit than he or she will ever deserve. In my opinion, there are really only **two reasons** that a narcissist acts the way he or she does on the game board of life *and both have to do with control*. In fact, everything that is confusing about how a narcissist thinks - why they do what they do and how easily is appears that they do it – can be attributed to this *control factor*. It's actually, just as my ex narcissist told me, quite simple.

Everything - and I mean *everything* - a narcissist's partner is subjected to during a relationship happens for one or both of the following: ***1) as a means of controlling that person, or 2) as a means for validating that control.*** That's it...that's all it is. Understand that *the relationship* only appears to be complicated because we choose to see it that way. The narc, in reality, isn't that complicated. The narcissist is simply doing what comes naturally for narcs...which is exactly what my ex meant when he said he was "a simple man". An action isn't complicated if you do it as naturally as brushing your teeth. Our suffering is caused by the relationship's perceived complexity. Therefore, we can eliminate the problem entirely by changing our perception! When I figured this out, my suffering was OVER.

A narcissist's main goal in the Game of Life is to control the emotions of other players so that he or she can reap whatever benefits may be provided. To "boot up" the relationship, the narcissist simply eases into it, gently mirroring our good qualities back to us. This occurs, of course, during the love-bombing stage and typically anytime the relationship is re-booted or reset in the years that follow. I like to describe this amazingly successful narcissistic tactic as *"creating the soul mate effect"*. As I explained earlier, these players are *imposters of the emotional kind* and they're very good at what they do. To achieve adoration, an ego boost, sex, or money, a narcissist will tell us *exactly* what we need to hear as if they can read our hearts and minds. Even when the narcissist is being 'good', he or she is controlling the situation; we simply don't know it. Once the goal is achieved, the narcissist starts a fight, creates chaos, cuts us loose, disappears, or subjects us to a silent treatment or cold shoulder. He or she will erase us as if we never meant a thing. These behaviors, while deliberate in nature, come naturally and, if successful, the expectations of partners are managed down in preparation for future go-rounds.

Ultimately, it is our reaction to this "managing down" process that *validates*, for the narcissist, that his or her control is as solid as a rock. Even when he or she disappears...when they literally are walking out the door...they will do it with confidence and feel no regret. **Understand that a narcissist doesn't care so much if they are with us physically as long as they are in our heads.** When a narcissist has taken us to the brink...to the point that he or she can actually *feel* our desperation and codependency, then the control is validated. The narcissist can go about his business secure in the fact that his now ex-partner will likely be around when and if he decides to show back up. And around and around the shit show goes. This particular control/validate process can happen in an hour, several times a day, over two weeks, or over many years. It's a push/pull system that translates to control/validate, control/validate, control/validate until we're ready to lose our minds, give up and give in. For the narc, it's simply a natural way to secure as many targets as possible for future narcissistic supply.

So, what appears to *us* to be meticulous and calculated planning of our demise is really just a narc either *controlling us* or *validating that control* in the situation. It doesn't get any simpler than that. If your narc is involved with other people, he will be validating the control there as well. While we go through our many gyrations...while we suffer needlessly...the narcissist never changes. I'm fairly convinced that this is all there is to it. As partners or ex-partners of these nefarious simpletons, we absolutely must stop over-thinking and over-analyzing these atrocious but natural (to the narcissist) behaviors. The control/validate process is one of the major key points to understanding the narcissist's psyche.

Mind you, my control/validate theory in no way pardons the narcissist for his or her despicable behaviors or for causing everyone, including their own children, so much pain. The narcissist is guilty as charged. I do believe that narcs like my ex really do believe in the simplicity of their own evil and this fact, once accepted, ultimately should validate how unfixable and unsustainable this type of psyche really is. Moreover, the fact that a narcissist's evil agenda is not nearly as complicated as we thought is very good news. It would mean that we no longer have to think so hard about *why* he or she does what they do. It means that we now need less of a reason to stay because we have one more very important reason to leave….to go No Contact…to get out of this very emotionally dangerous situation.

This book is about realizing it's time to save the rest of your life because *this person's **bad** is as **good** as it's ever going to get*. This book is about knowing, finally, that it's time to get out. An authentic life awaits once the toxic burden is released.

Chapter IV:
The Break-Up

With the right intention and the willingness to let a few things go, you can escape the bonds of your toxic lifestyle. You can choose to step off the game board and go back to square one with a clean slate or you can simply move away from the rouge players and win on your own. Either choice is just fine.

Now, the "rules" of breaking up with a narcissist are *completely different* than the rules that apply to even the most dysfunctional of "normal" relationship break-ups and this is actually great news. As a bonus, when you break up with a narcissist, there are a whole slew of typically inconvenient things that you simply *do not* have to worry about.

For example, when you decide to finally quit a narcissistic partner for good....

- You don't have to worry about hurting his feelings because he doesn't have any
- Because he's never around, you don't even have to *tell* him you're breaking up

- Even if you do break up in person, he'll likely be so insulted and ravaged by narcissistic injury that he'll start giving you the silent treatment anyway
- You don't have to worry about running into him anytime soon because of his Houdini-like ability to vanish off the face of the earth
- And so forth and so on…..

Of course, in order to *really* break up for good, there are a few things you will have to let go including:

- …the need to have the last word because it will ever happen. The narcissist is a *walking dictionary* of last words and he'll always have a better one.
- …the need to hear him confess and admit to every awful thing he's ever done to you because he won't have the slightest idea what you're talking about
- …the need to first get reimbursed for all the money you've either spent on him or he's "borrowed" from you because, again, he won't have the slightest idea what you're talking about
- …the need to have him grovel for forgiveness because, in the blink of an eye, he'll have *you* groveling for forgiveness and you won't even know how he did it
- …the need to break-up but *still* get closure-style revenge after the fact because chances are he's thought ahead and his revenge on *your* revenge will be much worse
- …and so forth and so on

Yes, ending a relationship with a narcissist is easier than you think because the reality is that you've been broken up the whole time! Just because the narcissist disappears *without saying a word* doesn't mean he hasn't broken up with you…because he *has*. Silent treatments are simply break-ups in disguise *intended* to make you *imagine* that the possibility that you haven't been dumped for good still exists. Whew!

Recently, I received a heartfelt email from a reader who wondered if 'No Contact' still counted if she decided to implement it during a silent treatment. Of course it counts! You can turn a narcissist's silent treatment around anytime just by saying *to yourself* "This is NOT a silent treatment. This is No Contact and I just dumped YOU!" In other words, since the narcissist is famous for disappearing or going cold, you can break up with him anytime simply by *not being there when he gets back or snaps out of it*. You can just as easily block HIS phone and change YOUR phone number - as he does to you - but you must do it with one thing being very, very different: **the intention.**

The silent treatment is a narcissist's way to avoid *you* dumping *him* by keeping you confused as to whether or not *he* just dumped *you*. He intends to return because his *intention* - always – is to keep you from moving on from the pain he has caused. He has, in fact, been moving on the entire time. You have to understand how the narcissist is thinking - the evilness and indifference of his plan - and accept it as truth. Because it is, in fact, the truth! Once you grasp the facts…that he doesn't and *has never* loved you, that he's perfectly happy playing this cat and mouse game forever, that he will never change and, therefore, wanting revenge and closure or to hear one more disingenuous "I'm sorry" is just a waste of precious time, it will become amazingly clear to you that dumping the narcissistic partner is far easier than you ever thought possible.

Now, when you co-parent with a narcissist, things are, of course, slightly different but only *technically* and I will discuss this in a later chapter. The truth is that narcissists are no better parents than they are partners. Narcissists walk out on their families to be with other partners all the time and don't have the slightest problem doing it. So, if you don't have the strength to end it while he's still living with you, simply wait for him to leave (and you know that, eventually, he *will)*, change the locks, tell the kids, and start the process of divorce.

I'm not saying that your decision to end it will not be sad. What I am saying is that if you stay focused and keep things in perspective, the actual break-up *isn't going to be that hard*. The hard part is always *within us* and it has to do with our inability to be honest with ourselves about the *intention* of the "break-up". If your plan, deep down, is to go No Contact in hopes that he will end his silent treatment, then simply wait for the hoover and save yourself the trouble. He's going to do all those awful things narcissists and sociopaths do whether you remain loyal to him or not. This is why going No Contact (NC), as hard as it appears to be in theory, is the only strategy that ever works.

Certainly, the concept of No Contact is nothing new for victims who have scoured the internet for answers. What makes it difficult is that we know that NC, by its true definition, means that this particular break-up is the last one. It means that you're willing to suffer a little heartache in exchange for a light at the end of the rabbit hole. It means ignoring any attempts by the narcissist to solicit a post break-up reaction. Going "No Contact" means that you, probably for the first time in a long time, are not willing to play this version of the Game of Life anymore. In essence, you are making a commitment to *yourself* to save your own sanity. Whether you can do all this without blaming yourself for participating is another question that I will address in this book. Many victims have a terrible time with this. I, for one, know you can do it. Again, it's all about perspective.

Chapter V:
Wanting to Believe

In my writings, I have said over and over that I don't subscribe to the victim blame-game. As a result, my ideas about what constitutes being labeled "co-dependent" are not the norm. To me, because of the weird dynamic of having a narcissistic partner, labeling ourselves as codependent or accepting the label from someone else (a therapist, etc.) can be dangerous as it only adds to our confusion, undermining the very process of recovery. Certainly we all have codependent *tendencies* but this doesn't make us "codependent" any more than the fact that we all have narcissistic tendencies (which we do) makes us each a narcissist. In these types of relationships, there are many mitigating circumstances!

My clients will ask "How could I have allowed this to happen?" or "Why did I stay? I'm so codependent!" or "OMG...I met narcissist #2. I need professional help!" I remember feeling all that too but here I am, almost six years later, and I'm okay. You will be too. While you may be reactionary, you are *not* crazy. I'm not saying that we shouldn't hold ourselves accountable for our behaviors during (and often after) the relationship, because of course we should. But only up to a point. Manipulative people are very good at what they do and it can happen to the best of us.

First of all, it is ***not*** abnormal for "normal" people like you and I to *want to believe* that the people we meet or engage with day to day are *telling us the truth* when they look into our eyes and speak. It is not abnormal for us to want to believe that the person that we love, even after doing hurtful things, *is actually sorry* if he or she is saying so. It's also not abnormal for us to want to believe that when this person that we love makes future plans with us that he or she will *actually follow through* and make it happen. None of that, to me, is abnormal even if we do it over and over. As you and I know, the narcissist understands human behavior and will count on the fact that **we always want to believe.**

The alternative to 'wanting to believe' is to exist in life assuming that each person we meet is lying to us until they prove otherwise and we're simply not going to do that. Thankfully, this is not human nature. It's not the way normal brains are wired. Right or wrong, it's not natural to assume, right off the bat, that the person speaking to us is a fake. The majority of "normal" people do not have their guard up 24/7. We count on our intuition to activate our bullshit meters and for the most part, when meeting the average person, this works. But the world isn't perfect and people with personality disorders do exist. As natural as it is for us to want to believe that people, as a whole, are good, it is just as natural for narcissists to happily use our own belief against us. So, how do we counter? I believe we counter best by developing emotional protective strategies that work within our "normal" parameters. It's not that difficult to be smarter than the average narcissist *now that we know that they exist...* and this brings us back the question of boundaries.

From: Annie

I was trying to think why narcs do what they do. It's like they have a master's degree in understanding human behavior and how to control people to do their bidding. What's most interesting is that it appears that all narcs somehow developed the same effective tactics & cycles to use as they wish to get what they want. Amazing.

Narcs act predatory in nature – like animals – and will develop the best and most effective ways to catch a meal. At the core of these

people is the fuel/supply that they need so badly to survive. In their minds, it's a life or death situation. Clearly, this fuel was never provided in a positive way from the narcissist's parents and they had to find other ways to extract it, often brutally, from those they meet later who come to care for and love them.

When the brain knows it needs something, it will seek out that which will provide it, even if the way it ultimately harnesses this power is inappropriate. The methods in which it will do this almost always involve the path of least resistance unless the human who owns this brain chooses to do differently. The brain will do what it needs to do to keep the body alive no matter what, even if this means shutting down empathy, guilt, love or compassion.

It comes down to choosing to do right over wrong. Since narcs have been predisposed to having no real moral compass, they will almost always choose to do the wrong thing even if the good thing will get them better results. This is why it appears that all narcs use the same tactics and behave the same way. As you say, Zari, they are nothing if not predictable. They stick to what they do and how they treat people because they know that it works. Plain and simple.

Many people who write or blog about narcissism make the claim that all targets, upon first meeting the narcissist, are basically boundary-free. They describe the "weaknesses" of narcissistic victims in detail, explaining that the narcissist feeds upon these insecurities. The target is, thus, easily conned into believing the lie. While certainly this thinking is true in some cases, it doesn't fit in with my own truth and with what I know to be true about narcissism in relationships. The boundary issue for a narcissist's target is just not that simple.

I have spoken and corresponded with hundreds of victims of narcissistic abuse and have never known a single one to be a wallflower. As a result, I have come to believe that narcissists are not even attracted to this type of person in the same way that narcissists are not attracted to other narcissists. The true romantic target of a narcissist has to fall somewhere in between. Gullible personalities simply present no challenge. To believe that only weak and gullible individuals become targets of emotional predators is just another way for psychologists and other mental health professionals to push victim blame and I don't buy into that.

When looking for a potential target, a narcissist will gravitate towards a person who, at least outwardly, exudes confidence. This is the person that a narc will ultimately want to break into pieces. Since everyone has some type of vulnerability somewhere, a narcissist will dig deep to find it by being very attentive and "concerned" during initial conversations. Almost everything you say in confidence to a narcissist will come back to bite you, even if it takes years. As I've said before, my ex bragged about his ability to "read a person in five minutes". He would say it with a smirk, acting quite proud of himself. Clearly, only a narc thinks like this but we certainly don't assume that this is the mindset of everyone we meet. So, if, in retrospect, we appeared to have lacked boundaries at the start, it is likely because we never felt the need to break them out or put them up in previous relationships. In fact, most of us are not aware that we lack a boundary until the narcissist crosses one that wasn't there. For good or bad, we want to believe that most people are good shut the "bullshit" detector off. This isn't the crime that certain people who speak about narcissism make it out to be. Being "normal" is not a crime.

When I became the narc's girlfriend, I was at a very good place in my life. I had a good job, good friends, and I enjoyed a quasi-celebrity status as the singer in a popular rock band. A prior romantic relationship had ended amicably and I was dating around, partying, and generally having a great time. Since I had known the narcissist for a decade already as a friend and fellow musician, I thought our new and improved "friendship" was nothing less than a bonus in my great life. *Who needed boundaries?* As the narc's "friend", I ignored he red flags of his behavior around others because he wasn't my boyfriend. Of that, I am guilty. Those of us who know nothing about the narcissistic personality have no reason to assume that anyone we meet – let alone someone we thought we already knew - will have one. It would be wonderful if narcs wore t-shirts that read, "I'M A NARCISSIST. FOR YOUR OWN EMOTIONAL SAFETY, KEEP WALKING" but they do not. And even if they did, we'd probably find this shirt intriguing and opt to engage anyway because…well…that's the kind of people we are! Life is full of harsh lessons.

Yes, despite what others may say, what you might read, and what you might even believe yourself, it's likely that you *weren't* a lackluster wallflower wallowing in low self-esteem when you hooked up with the narc. We typically feel *good* when we meet this person and toss caution to the wind even if something seems "off". Perhaps you shared a common interest, as I did with my ex, which he or she, in turn, utilizes in self-serving ways. During the love-bombing stage, the narcissist magically transforms the things that *you* enjoy into things that you suddenly enjoy *together*. Later, of course, these commonalities become the catalyst for feelings of jealousy and insecurity that you may have never felt before. You become confused at the change within your own psyche. In my case, the initial musical connection I felt with my ex was amazing. But soon enough, through various covert means, he soon tipped my love for music upside down. I felt threatened and jealous and I didn't know why. It's a very clever trick, this bait and switch. To someone who has never loved a narc, this sounds paranoiac and absurd. To those of us who know, it makes perfect sense.

Some ask why narcissists go to the trouble of scoping out only those targets that they must "break" when there are certainly wallflower targets available who are already broken. My answer to this simple: *To a narcissist, life is simply not fun if there is no one's confident back behind which to do evil things.* It is all about the challenge. My ex, during snippets of truth, would admit this to me many times. During this period of my 'great' life, I inadvertently neglected to create relationship deal-breakers and boundaries. I never had any reason to before. During previous relationships that ended badly, I never felt that my "boundaries" had even been crossed. So, when the narcissist crosses personal boundaries that we didn't even know that we had, the feeling is nothing less than inexplicable pain. We can't for the life of us understand *why* we feel such *grief*. The *depth of the betrayal* is so beyond our comprehension that we stay around just to figure it out...*to see what could possibly happen next*. Many women and men I speak with will admit that, initially, they had little interest in the narc...that he or she wasn't even their type. Soon after the initial contact, they could have easily walked way. Then, in the blink of a narcissistic eye, the entire dynamic flipped. Oh *yeah, that's right*...it's what they do.

If you are reading or listening to this book, clearly you know that the fallout from your relationship is going to be – or already is - a heap of collateral mental damage. The narcissist's mindset, however, in his or her attempt to win at the Game of Life, must keep you. Narcissists will accomplish this through clever deception, distraction, and interception. The relationship will not end until the narcissist is ready and can call the shots. Even with the signs coming fast and furious, you will find it difficult to navigate the rabbit hole. Intellectually, you "get it", but there is still that nagging question in the back of your mind about your own participation. After all, the narcissist will always concur that you are the problem. You simply cannot buy into this 'projection' madness.

To stay on the path, we have to accept the many reasons *why* it has to end. We have to turn around and make the lonely trip back because the only way out is from whence we came! It doesn't have to traumatizing because the signs of the end have been there all along. We simply did not choose to see. So, open your eyes….this is a time of recovery and we are just getting started.

Chapter VI:
Signs of the End

So, what are those signs that we've been ignoring since almost day one? To start, let's talk about the sustainability factors of the relationship. Guess what? There aren't any! When you feel the separation anxiety, simply remember this as fact. Ask yourself if anything about your situation is *sustainable*. And by 'sustainable', I mean good for the long-term. *Anyone can make a situation sustainable day to day but how about for the future?* When you look ahead even one year, what do you see?

Below is my list of what I believe to be universal reasons for implementing No Contact. I consider this list to be, when we're involved with a deceptive partner, the most blatant signs of the end times to come.

You know it is time to end the relationship when:

- *....the end of your relationship is never-ending. In other words, it ends a lot but, in reality, it never* ends. *He is always leaving you – whether via silent treatment as punishment (a break-up in disguise), accusatory projection, rouge disappearance for no reason at all, or simply bad behavior in general. It's time to call it quits.*

- *...you can't let go, no matter how bad this person treats you. You may desire to let go and may even put your foot down periodically, but the truth is that your intention of escaping is fleeting. You find yourself addicted to the very drama that you hate. The narcissist knows this, of course, because he has created it. He will accept the vacation with a smirk and wait for you to grovel back. It's time to stop this ridiculous insanity.*

- *...you've become a booty call, a buddy fuck, a friend with benefits, or however you'd like to describe it. The truth, however, is that this person leaves you, lies to you, hurts you, abuses you, neglects you, abandons you, cheats on you, and STILL gets to sleep with you. How is this a win-win? It is not.*

- *...except for the beginning stages, you've never felt part of a couple. Either you do nothing together at* *all or he's made a point to have an entirely separate life where he does plenty without you. When we don't feel part of a couple with the person we love, we know it. It hovers in the background like a dark cloud. The narc manages down our expectations of the relationship so that we accept that which is completely disrespectful.*

- *...you've become a super-sleuth, a master investigator, a private-eye extraordinaire when it comes to uncovering "the truth" yet you can't seem to get to the bottom of anything. There is always more to uncover and more things to find out. What you've really become is an expert at wasting your own time and, as a result, your life is slowly slipping away. No one should ever make you feel suspicious 100% of the time – ever! It's time to stop the cycle of your own abuse to yourself.*

- *...you cry more than you smile. No need to elaborate further.*

- *...the needs of your children are starting to interfere with your obsession time and, even though you know this, you can't stop the feeling that you just* *want the kids to go away so that you can ruminate, investigate, and/or wait for the narcissist's call in peace.*

- *...you've inadvertently, and even deliberately, become not only a stalker and a snoop, you've become one of those partners that gets down on their hands and knees begging for forgiveness just to keep the peace...even when the issue at hand was no fault of your own. If you do this even once (and we have all done it a thousand times!), the show, unfortunately, must come to an end.*

- *.....you find yourself willing to forgive just about anything just to eliminate or avoid separation anxiety. Your gut tells you he cheats (even if you haven't been able to prove it) and yet you take him back. He disappears and reappears with completely illogical excuses yet you open the door. He'll go for long stretches without texting or calling but you will jump through hoops when the phone rings. If you do miss a call, all hell will break loose. The rules are completely different for the narcissist than they are for you in this particular Game of Life...and you allow it.*

Any one or all of the above sound familiar? They sure do to me. To put up with all or even one of the above scenarios is ridiculous. Do you understand this? When the "love" that we feel becomes all about the suffering that we endure, a decision has to be made. With the narcissist, 'love' might have been a lie, but this is not YOUR crime. Do not spend time on non-productive self-blame. Believing in the goodness of people is not a crime and manipulative people are good at what they do. To experience real love, we have to separate from the madness. We owe ourselves this and so much more. There is no way to secure an authentic life unless you submerse yourself in truth. If you stay in a toxic relationship, you will always feel a certain type of emotional sickness that will send you down the wrong path. It's a form of trauma-based mind control. We must remove those people from our life that have the *wrong intention.*

Now, I'll be the first to say that there are certain people in our past – former boyfriends, girlfriends, husbands, and wives – that do not deserve to be cut out of our lives forever and maybe not at all. Somewhere down the road, after the pain has passed and time has healed our wounds, rekindling a friendship with certain people is entirely possible. The narcissist, however, does not fall into this category.

An ex who is a narcissist, in his or her attempt to coax you out of No Contact, may attempt to play the "friend" card. He or she will make it appear, quite convincingly, that it is entirely possible for the two of you to break up and remain buddies. Logically, how could this ever be a possibility? The narcissist was never your friend to begin with. Remaining 'friends' with a narcissist does nothing more than keep targets attached to the problem. We will always be the *only one* in the arrangement extending any wisps of friendship. Inevitably, we wake one morning to the familiar pangs of anxiety and by lunchtime, we'll already staring at the phone, letting all other calls go to voicemail. The silence once again becomes deafening. Soon, we begin the 'power calling' cycle, ringing the narc's number over and over while, at the same time, berating ourselves for making something out of nothing. Yet, we can't stop. When the narc finally picks up - and they will - we hear the infamous question: "What the hell is your problem?" Flustered, we whimper quietly that everything seemed fine yesterday so why no call or text today. To that, the narc remains silent for five terrifying seconds before responding calmly, with just a touch of smugness, "Well, I really don't have to call you at all. Don't you remember? We're just friends now." And then the door to the rabbit hole slams shut.

Yes, to consider being a "friend with benefits" to your narcissistic ex is a brutal mistake and completely illogical. We do it in the hopes that the narcissist will only be sleeping with *us* during the break-up but this is never the case. If we continue the cycle, the damage to our psyche can becomes nearly irreparable. Do not allow this to happen. The only one who benefits from this type of 'friendly' sexual arrangement is the narcissist since the truth is that he's *not* just sleeping with you. Now, post break-up, due to "the arrangement", he or she gets to do it all. Do not be delusional about this fact just because the sex is or was exceptional (if it was). I had exceptional sex each and every time for 13 years with my ex and I always thought this was the glue that held us together. It was not. To a narcissist, great sex is great sex. There is no mental connection on the narcissist's part to anyone. This is how they do what they do and feel justified doing it. This is why they feel no remorse and no regret.

Intellectually, I know you understand all this but the *mental connection* we have to this false love is strong and persistent. We have to break the tether to this toxicity and only the target can do it. Contrary to what the narc may tell you, your obsession and reactionary behavior within the relationship is NOT his ball and chain. He *likes* the toxic connection because it *validates his control*. Understand the game and how it is played and you *will* eventually let go of the madness. It becomes a matter of fight or flight and, in some cases, even life or death.

So, how can we break the mental connection? In my search for answers, I came across some very interesting information. There is actually a name for this twisted attachment that, on some level, further confirms for me that the strength of our connection to narcissistic abusers is simply not our fault….and it's called *trauma bonding*.

Chapter VII:
Trauma Bonding

Feeling attached to a narcissist even though he or she treats us badly is a constant source of angst for anyone trying to recover from this type of relationship. We demand to know **why**...*why can't I just let go? Why can't I move on? Why do I feel so connected to someone who feels no connection to me?* One logical explanation for this is that we're normal and *they're not* and normal people want to fix things that are broken so that they work again *in the same manner that they did before.* The problem is that a narcissist can't be fixed because he or she was never right to begin with. What a narcissist lacks that makes him or her "different" cannot be re-created in any way. And even if it could, the narcissist wouldn't be interested. In essence, narcissists like themselves just the way that they are. This, of course, is a very big problem.

So, what do we do, after a discard, when we can't shake the feeling of being only half a person...when we can't shake the feeling of being disconnected yet, at the same time, utterly attached? As we know, this feeling can occur – as illogical as it seems – even when we know for sure this person is with someone else. Well, there *is* an answer to this question for those who seek a deeper psychological – and even physiological - reason for the suffering and it's a condition often referred to as *trauma bonding.*

Trauma bonding is typically associated with The Stockholm Syndrome (TSS) – a condition named after an event that occurred in Sweden in the 70's where a group of hostages became so emotionally attached to their kidnapers that they refused to testify against them in court after the rescue. Trauma bonding now refers to this particular type of emotional attachment. In essence, the term describes the type of trauma that a toxic partner such as a narcissist can cause to our *emotions (i.e.* **betrayal and neglect***, over and over and over).* It's the type of relationship bonding that can easily occur via passive-aggressive manipulation (i.e. sex, lies, manipulation, and silent treatments) and other forms of narcissistic control.

From: Moving On

I met my N last April and dated him until the end of August when I became fed up with all his lies. A week later, he rented out the house next to mine and a week after that, I discovered that I was pregnant. I decided to make a go of things for the sake of our child, but the pregnancy was horrible and I was sick the whole time. During my sixth month, I attempted to discuss my fears about our becoming parents but just five sentences into the discussion, he screamed, "If you can't trust me, we are over!" I continued to hang on and gave birth prematurely a month and a half later. He helped out very little and went about his life, finding other women. That summer, I gave the ultimatum that is was me or his other girlfriend and he chose her and has been with her ever since. He brings her by his house (next door!) constantly and flaunts her kids every chance he gets, playing with them on his front yard and even babysitting, etc. while only spending the court ordered 2 hours per week with our daughter. At our child support hearing, he had said he would be moving out at the end of his lease, but here it is September and he has done no such thing.

While I am grateful I did not end up with him, he is still my neighbor. I use our lawyers for communication and never let on that him living next door irritates or bothers me. Even using the lawyers, I feel stuck in my recovery. During normal break ups, you don't have to see your ex every single day. I am lost on how to get the mental space needed to move on fully and would love whatever advice I can get. I can't break this mental connection.

Dear Moving On,

Girl, I hope your ex moves away because I am at a loss as to what to tell you to do that you haven't already been doing. When I respond to letters, the first thing that I do is put myself in the shoes of the person writing and your shoes, I must admit, make me very uncomfortable. How the hell do you do it? I can't even imagine *having to live next door to that monster because I know exactly how he thinks and, yes, I have no doubt he is flaunting his life in front of you. I am also shocked that his new "girlfriend" would even be okay with the situation...what kind of girl would do that and what has he told her that would even convince her that any of it – ANY of it – is okay?*

Now, having said all that, let's figure out what your options are. Given the fact that you still live there, I am assuming that you own this house or are in the process of owning it (have a mortgage), right? If you were only renting, I would think that you would have moved out long ago to get away from such a horrible situation. Is it at all possible for you to perhaps rent out your house for a few months (on a month-to-month basis or short-term lease) until he leaves? Or perhaps, do you have a close friend who lives in a decent/convenient area who would swap with you? I know it sounds crazy but I can GUARANTEE that if you leave that house, he will also leave because he is ONLY living there to ruin your life and the life of that baby. It's none of his business where you move to or why you are leaving or who lives in the house while you are not there so it's not as if you owe him an explanation at all. Believe me, I understand that to do any of this with a baby is overwhelming but, My God!, what choice do you have?

Other than the above, I have to say that not letting the bastard know how you feel about him being right next door is all you can do. Personally, I would be a lunatic and probably to the point that he would leave on his own just to get away from me. That, of course, could be your other option. SHOW him and his girl how much you hate it and he just might leave overnight. Right now, it's all too easy for him to stay there. He only has to walk next door for a two-hour visit and the rest of the time, since you act normally, he gets to fantasize about how miserable he is making you. Maybe you should give him what he wants. Turn it around. Make him sorry for what he wishes for. Other than that, girl, I would find a way to get out of that house. How much do you really love it? Is it worth your sanity to stay there? This is what you have to figure out.

The narcissistic partner is very shrewd in his *understanding of the pathological behavioral process* that streamlines a victim's codependency to the point of least resistance. Narcissists have figured out – without a single day of formal training - that the most effective way to ensnare narcissistic supply is to create trauma bonds with his or her target via the method of *seduce and discard.*

The conditioning that leads to trauma bonding involves a combination play (on the Life game board) of two powerful sources of reinforcement called the *'arousal-jag"*. In order to work perfectly, this powerful combination reoccurs in succession over and over and at perfectly timed intervals. The first source is the *'arousal'* which refers to the *excitement before the trauma* and the second source is the 'jag' which refers to *the peace of surrender* that occurs afterwards. Take a second to reflect on the narcissist's behaviors. Creating trauma bonds through this type of reinforcement is what narcissists have been doing their entire lives.

'Arousal-jag' reinforcement is all about *giving a little* and then *taking it away* over and over and over in *well timed, perfectly spaced intervals*. Narcissists do this in a variety of ways that are conducive to typical narcissistic habits such as disappearing and reappearing and creating chaos and then going silent. These habits create illusions of twisted excitement that reinforce the traumatic bond between us and them. And to be clear, the narcissist *does* feel a connection to us here as well but it is different. The connection is not what we imagine it is or what they make it appear to be. The connection felt by a narcissist is to the excitement alone and we serve as the catalyst. This is why a narcissist keeps multiple partners…because in doing so, the excitement factor is doubled and tripled. The fact that we, along with the others, become so attached to the chaos that we will await his or her return is quite an added bonus!

Are you getting it yet? Stay with me here because I'm gearing up for a punch line.

The excitement before the trauma (arousal) is created during the devalue stage. This is the point right before a discard when our intuition has already told us the narc is going to leave. Certain recognizable behaviors are offered as clues. Remember, we're playing a Game here. This happened to me too many times to count. As crazy as it sounds, there was a way my ex would play with his phone, fiddling with it all day long while claiming it wasn't working properly, that let me know that it would soon be turned off. Of course, he would deny this accusation when confronted but I knew what was coming. I had been there many times before. The knot-in-my-stomach feeling when he was with me would develop into an overwhelming urge to call his phone over and over when he was away or to write letter upon letter begging him not to do whatever I knew he was planning to do.

The 'arousal' reinforcement is the feeling we get from the darkness - or drama - that a narcissist deliberately creates right before the storm. And, unfortunately, this drama – the very drama that we've always claimed to hate - can be very addicting.

So, once the 'arousal' reinforcement has occurred to the narcissist's liking, everything goes silent. And not only do we actually begin to miss the chaos, we miss it *terribly*. This *aloneness* makes us hate our own behaviors and feelings. We *long* for the connection, as manipulated and fabricated as that connection may be. Sometimes, we can barely breathe. Then, seconds before our breaking point, in he or she swoops once again, seemingly up from the ashes like a Phoenix rising. With this return, we are given our second reinforcement: *the 'jag' or peace of surrender that happens afterwards.*

The narcissist's reappearance is meticulously timed for maximum impact and will usually follow a silent treatment that has gone on just a tad longer than the one before. The narcissist is conditioning us to accept less and less so that he or she can get away with more each disappearance.

Like it or not, this second dose of reinforcement feels absolutely like heaven! Again, it's an addiction, but it's like any other and it's simply no good. This time around, we wallow in the make-up sex, the vanishing of our anxiety, and the feeling of calmness and euphoria we get from *once again* being given *a reprieve to breathe* until the cycle repeats again. Seduce and discard…seduce and discard….the rinse and repeat of a vicious cycle. Back down the rabbit hole we go to that place where we believe we belong. And, in that moment, we're okay with all of it. In fact, there's no place else we'd rather be and nothing in the world we'd rather be doing.

Since the final break-up with my ex, I have come to realize the amount of work he put into my trauma bonding. At one point, my silent treatments ran two weeks on/ two weeks off like clockwork for months at a time and with no explanation. I said nothing and did nothing except weep like a fool until he returned. Then, to compound the insanity, from mid-October until January 2nd, he'd make like Houdini and fall completely off the grid. He did this almost every year for 13 years. In October, before he left, he would ramp up the chaos, making me feel anxious and angry about his suspicious behaviors. He played along, creating the 'arousal' reinforcement while telling me I was crazy and over-sensitive. I was trauma bonded to all of it and he knew it. This guy knew *exactly* what he was doing!

From: Heather

Your book has helped to make sense of what I was going through for 10 years. Like so many others, I have lost so many years to a narcissist and this hurts. However, I finally have an understanding as to who these people are. Like others, I met this guy at work, a place I thought was pretty safe for meeting someone. I had just come out of an abusive marriage. He treated me like a princess and I felt my prayers had been answered. Before long, he was whisking me off on a romantic trip to Paris – a trip where I witnessed the first of his rages over something trivial. This was followed by several hours of a silent treatment. Of course, how was I to know right then that he was setting the stage for a relationship filled with gas lighting, silent treatments, abuse and punishments?

Next came more holidays to faraway places, a new car, and even, like a scene from Pretty Woman, a day where he bought me a complete new wardrobe. The gifts were endless and I worried how he could afford to spend so much money. Eventually, although the weekends away continued, he started to want his mother to join us on these holidays. I never questioned why but now, looking back, I see that she was there to provide him endless narcissistic supply whilst behind closed doors, he could abuse me, turning his back on me in bed and allowing his mother to believe that it was me who was in the wrong.

He was hard to get close to and I always felt him pull away if he thought I wasn't giving him attention or if I criticized him in any way. I began to feel paranoid as if there was another love interest. Sexually, he would pull away, making me feel like I wasn't doing it for him anymore. He preferred masturbation to a loving night in bed together and I felt myself trying hard to hold on. I found his picture on dating sites yet he denied it. I found women's fashion magazines in his car but he claimed to have no knowledge as to how they got there. I began doubting every story, questioning him about everything. Behind closed doors, I researched bipolar disorder and abusive relationships looking for answers. He spoke of being neglected as a child so I tried to love him more to gain his trust and ease his "insecurity".

During this time, my job took me out of town for training and I dreaded telling him of the schedule. He insisted on coming along, claiming that he was scared of losing me, yet hardly showed affection on the trip. He would phone me constantly and demanded I answer even if I was in a meeting. He hated being ignored. I was jumping through hoops for this guy and the goalposts kept moving.

I wanted to escape but the good days we occasionally shared kept me hooked and I didn't know what to do. He would abandon me in restaurants, dump me in the middle of town at night, cut me off from my family and friends and allow no contact with anyone on social media. My life was a living hell and my nerves were shattered. I felt scared. I was literally riding on a roller coaster that simply wouldn't stop.

Vacancy In the Rabbit Hole

It was not abnormal for him to text me up to 60 times per day and, if I went missing, to have the same amount of calls. In the end, I dreaded going out the door and doing anything that gave me pleasure like going to the gym and socializing. To do anything, I had to have his approval and permission and, even then, he'd be moody with further silent treatments given as punishment.

I made excuses for him all the time. He had lost endless jobs and accumulated over 30K in debts that he couldn't pay or even explain. Since we were planning on buying a house together, I was always asking questions. When he complained about having no money, I took him to New York to cheer him up and away for weekends. Things had reversed financially. Since he had always seemed so giving, his debt worried me but it was clear to see he had nothing to offer and no equity in his home. Supposedly, he had remortgaged his home twice to clear his son's private school fee which had been passed on to him in his divorce. Even though he said it was he who initiated the divorce, I thought it odd that his wife had had to get a barrister involved to get away from him.

Finally, a job offer came through and he was so excited that he whisked me off on holiday with his mother in tow. Although full of romance, he still pulled away when I tried to get close to him in bed at night. That was our last holiday together as he pulled the plug when we got home, saying he wasn't happy and that the relationship wasn't working. Within a matter of months, I found a picture of him and his new woman on his football website at a trophy presentation event.

I am 12 months out of the fog now. Honestly, I had to hit rock bottom before I could fully understand what had been going on. I never knew what a narcissist was but now, having been "chosen" to go through this journey, I am now a stronger person. My days are quiet without him but I finally have a chance to breathe and rebuild my life. It's still early though and I know this. At times it feels like it was all a dream........

From: Me

Hi Heather,

Thank you so much for sharing your story and I am so glad that you are away from this man. I must say that bringing the mother on the trips was very bizarre but that your idea about why he did it was spot-on. While strange, it is still the typical odd behavior becoming of a narc. Although others reference many different kinds of narcs, I see only two - the high-level narc and the low-level narc - and the only difference between the two is money. Other than that, they are exactly the same. Yours, for the most part, had money and mine did not but - man oh man - so much of what you described struck a chord right down to the odd dynamic with his mother, the punishments, the abandonment in restaurants and being dumped on the side of the rode in town in the dark, the texting and jumping through hoops at work in the middle of meetings - OMG. For me, sex was the hook...for you, the few good times...all of it mere crumbs of what we truly deserved.

I wish you nothing but the best and I'm grateful that you still visit my site to read and post. Stay strong sister and know that your life is all your own now. Make every day Silence Appreciation Day.

Our addiction to the chaos and *then to the reprieve* also explains why we find it so hard to move on into other relationships after it's over. No one excites us in quite the same way or with the same intensity as the toxic partner. Via trauma bonding, *we become the suffering and the suffering becomes us.* I will discuss this further in Chapter 10. We forget what normalcy feels like. The chaos and turmoil becomes almost as big a turn-on for us as it does for the narcissist.

But here's the kicker to this whole chapter – the punchline I had promised - and some of you may already know this little tidbit. This will be relevant to the women reading but the men should find it fascinating as well. It's actually a scientific fact that *women are biologically susceptible* to trauma bonding...and it all has to do with a bonding hormone (actual term!) called Oxytocin. Yes, that's right, there appears to be a biological reason why we so easily become addicted to the narcissistic nonsense. While this doesn't completely excuse our susceptibility, I found it nonetheless interesting. Oxytocin is the actual chemical that starts the birth process...the chemical that, by preventing *memory consolidation,* allows us to forget the pain of childbirth to the point that we'll actually choose to have *more* children. I found this fact to be absolutely amazing. This may partly explain why we continue to take the narc back or why we may even move on to find narcissist number two and three.

The prevention, biologically, of memory consolidation is very similar in nature to the phenomena that I discuss in the next chapter and refer to as *relationship amnesia.* By my definition, relationship amnesia is our ability to forget the narcissist's bad behaviors almost as soon as we're apart from this person. *Relationship amnesia* is part of the mental connection that keeps us addicted and oxytocin, apparently, is part of the reason it happens. However, while an adorable baby is our reward for the pain of childbirth, there is no reward for the pain caused by a narcissist abuser. Therefore, this information is provided only as an interesting side note and not as an excuse for why we're here.

Trauma bonding is created by a very clever captor to keep his victim co-dependent. It is all part of the evil that is narcissism and one of the biggest reasons why we must, at some point, commit to No Contact. It always comes back to that.

As a break-up strategy, No Contact is as powerful as it is *because* of the trauma bonding. It works because our ongoing post-break-up mental connection with and to the narcissistic partner is over-the-top. If we want any semblance of normalcy, we simply must *break the connection.* It is not extreme to compare your attachment to the narc with that of a drug addict to a drug because, as both and you and I know, it certainly feels like the worst kind of addiction. When the narc reappears after a vanishing or silent treatment, there is a kind of quasi-high or emotional rush that feels like an instant awakening...like receiving a sudden fix after an opiate withdrawal. The fog miraculously lifts. All of the anxiety goes away and we can actually laugh and smile. No matter what the narcissist did while away, the weight that lifts when he or she reappears makes it all worthwhile. And even then, with the reprieve in place, it ain't no walk in the park. People with drug addictions go to rehab facilities to get this shit done and *we have to do it on our own.*

Up until the point of the hoover or return, our mental connection peaks. We feel tethered to the toxicity. The bonds *are* traumatic and they *are* real. We are likely inconsolable, heart-sick, and consumed with thoughts of the relationship and where it went wrong. Rumination (our obsessive thoughts) are invasive and crippling and nothing but a dose of the narc can fix it. I was always my skinniest self during a silent treatment because I couldn't eat a bite and even if I did, my anxiety was the ultimate fat burner. Literally, my nerve endings were on fire all of the time. Again, nothing about this break-up is going to be normal because nothing about the relationship and the type of abuse involved is sane in any sense of the word.

The breaking of the mental connection must be front and

center in the break-up strategy and this is why the act of blocking a narc's number, whereby making it impossible for this person to call or text, is so powerful. Trust me, I hear from many men and women who have gone NC and find this "blocking" technique to be the most uncomfortable. They will explain that, after beginning NC, they find themselves ruminating on whether he's texting or not texting or calling or not calling. I will listen to this for a minute and then ask, "Well, have you blocked him? Because if you block him, you won't have to worry about any of that." Seriously, for as simple as it sounds, when I say this, light bulbs flick on. The next time I hear from these people, they're amazed at how peaceful the silence is and their only regret is that they hadn't done it sooner.

What we don't realize while we're in the relationship (and right after we get out of it) is the sheer magnitude of the time we actually spend waiting on the narc's next move. We're either waiting for a text or a call or for him to come over or whatever. To keep us in a constant state of heightened anxiety is the intention of each and every strategy in the narcissist's pathological relationship agenda. These strategies, obviously, are as deliberate as they are effective. When we actually make a move to block this person from being able to implement his evil, life miraculously begins to change. Suddenly, we can do whatever we want whenever we want. All the reasons for our rumination and intrusive thoughts and all the time spent waiting in limbo is eradicated. How many times have you postponed or simply not done something you needed or wanted to do because of your anxiety over missing the narc's calls

Vacancy In the Rabbit Hole

or texts? How many sleepless nights have you endured while imagining the inevitable punishment to come? Believe me, the "block" will set you free!

Chapter VIII:
Relationship Amnesia

Whatever you may feel about the narcissist in your life, it's important to know that he/she didn't get this way overnight. Our brain often refuses to believe this. I see this with clients who adamantly insist that they were blind-sided by certain narcissistic behaviors. The source of their pain is a false belief that they never saw it coming. *I don't get it! He (or she) wasn't like this for the first five years of the marriage (or relationship). I'm shocked!* However, they can say this all they want and I will never be convinced. I ask them to think back and think hard…to take off the rose-colored glasses of (what I call) **relationship amnesia** and really reflect. The truth is that the narcissistic signs have always been there. It might *feel* to us that we've been blind-sided but deep down we absolutely know better.

As I explain in *When Love Is a Lie*, I didn't begin to google my ex's behaviors until almost eight years in. Only then did I have the "a-ha" moment of WHO and WHAT he really was and turn into a piece of jelly. *How could I have not seen this? What the fuck is going on? Am I or was I completely blind?* No, of course I wasn't blind...I just didn't want to see. This blindness can continue on even after we know the truth. If left alone, it will evolve into an amnesia that only allows us to remember the very few good qualities that actually made the narc appear normal. We'll remember the times he or she made us laugh, the great sex, or the moment of apparent clarity where the narc appeared to actually care about us. The brutal truth is that all those memories mean absolutely *nothing* if the narcissist doesn't or didn't have your back as a loving partner. And they never do.

There comes a time in the relationship, somewhere near the end, that even the narcissist knows the jig is up. For example, say that you and the narc have been involved for ten years and you're just now finding out he's been cheating for the past two. This is a devastating discovery, obviously. Your narc, however has suddenly become horribly mean and nasty, basically blaming YOU for the fact that he's been busted. Maybe for the initial minute, he actually appeared sorry. However, now, a few days later, he not only offers little or no remorse for what he did, he apparently has zero tolerance or compassion for your feelings about it. This happened to me several times and I hear about it every day during consultations. The loving partner feels absolutely shell shocked. *Why isn't he sorry?* OR *Why isn't he MORE sorry? How could this happen...we've been great together all this time!* The truth is that no, you *haven't* been great at all but relationship amnesia and denial kicks in immediately. The truth is that the narcissist likely has been cheating or *working* on cheating or *preparing* to cheat the entire time that you've been together. *Oh, that's impossible. We were together 24/7. He didn't have time to cheat.* Oh, yes he did. Narcissists have nothing BUT time when it comes to planning for their next meal. However, now the jig is finally up – the jig that has been going on behind your back for years – and this is truly an inconvenient time for the falsely entitled narcissist. His tolerance for your pain fades quickly. As partners, we have to face the fact that we've been conned since the very first date.

When we focus on the "good" times post-break-up, we are viewing the relationship through a manipulated reality. Relationship amnesia can keep us stuck on stupid during a time where we could be moving forward in our recovery. Sure, things *appeared* to be "okay" for years but, believe me, it was only as "okay" as the narcissist allowed.

Indeed, the love-bombing stage happens quickly because the narcissist is working his butt off to *get it over with* so that you can be on the hook and he can do what he wants. This is why things feel so intense so early on…but intensity and love are not interchangeable. So, five years down the road, while you've been looking the other way to keep the peace, trying your best to not appear needy or jealous, he (or she) has been going about his narcissistic business, fulfilling the requirements of the relationship agenda. This is the truth!

Partners of narcs always suspect things but rarely find the evidence to convict and the punishments for trying to figure it out, as much as they hurt, become part of the routine and the next thing you know, five years has gone by. None of it was "great" – not a single damn thing. When and if we do decide to leave and even if the narcissist leaves us, if we truly want to recover from the pain, we have to accept this. We have to be confident *in the truth that we know* even when it hurts. The relationship with your narcissist has been over since day one. Don't allow relationship amnesia to whisper to you differently. You're smarter than that!

And, let me tell you, when the jig is up, it is *up*. The mask falls never to be worn again. The narc won't even pick it up; he just steps right over it and moves along. No more Mr. Nice Guy. Narcissists who've been busted and become raging angry have, without a doubt, been doing it forever! *This is why they're so fucking angry.* Life has suddenly become inconvenient and the narc will let you know it. A normal person who cheats and gets caught will typically feel guilty that he or she has hurt the loving partner. Then, this normal person may choose to stay with his partner/spouse or choose to go, but either way he will do it with a TRUE guilty conscience. This is how normal people play the Game of Life. He or she will tolerate the crying jags, the jealousy, the accusations, and the "fuck you's" because they know that they have *done you wrong*. A narcissist never feels this way. He just feels pissed. He will not exchange a Conscience card. Remember, with a narc, it's all about what he (or she) can get away with all day, every day. To you, the disruption feels shocking and sudden but the truth is that your nefarious partner has been doing what they do a very long time. This "bad" side of this person that you love is who he or she really is and who he or she has always been.

I tell a little story in my second book, **_Stop Spinning, Start Breathing_**, about such a situation…

Then there was the time, about six years later, that ex, after cheating on me, getting caught, having no choice but to admit to it, and then trying everything - including smacking me on the head - to pull me out of my crying jag, finally realized he might have gone too far. Feigning remorse, he begged me to forgive him. I continued to sob, pleading "Why? Why? Why did you do it?" until the narc, unable to pretend a second longer, threw up his hands in exasperation and yelled, "I don't know! I always figured I could do whatever I wanted and you'd still take me back!"

To truly recover and find peace…to heal our sad and fractured heart…we have to accept the brutality of the relationship in its entirety. We must push through the delusional nostalgia of relationship amnesia and get back to the business of life. By understanding and accepting that the relationship was *never* great, we can actually skip the grieving process when the nonsense is finally over. In my opinion, as I will discuss later, we can skip the forgiveness too. *No, not that! How can I heal if I don't forgive?* We don't have to forgive because we simply don't have the spiritual credentials to forgive at that level! This is very good news as I will explain.

Look, we can't grieve the loss of something we never had, my friends. The narcissist did not become a narcissist overnight and no amount of bittersweet amnesia is going to change that. He (or she) was born that way or raised that way and he (or she) will now always be that way. You, fortunately, are not doomed to the same fate because you are everything he or she is not.

Indeed, you *are perfect just the way that you are.* We *can* break our addiction to the toxic bonds that narcissists and sociopaths create. We *can* ignore the pull of a fading memory even if we're swimming in Oxytocin. Our power is in our self-worth and too many women and men base their personal self-worth on another person's bad behaviors. Let's give that a little thought…

Chapter IX:
Logical Self-Worth

Wow….the mind is a very powerful thing and we must learn to ignore it! When we are with a narcissist or when we are apart, we can create an entire world in our heads and become absolutely insane. When my ex and I were "apart", I would sit at my desk and just think – and I mean hard. My brain could think up some crazy scenarios and I could literally, in my mind, bring them to life. If the scenarios in my head (which are always crazier than the truth), had come to life, I'm might have killed myself or HIM, who knows! Nonetheless, I could sit with my thoughts and feel myself in the situation or feel the situation happening. I imagined the narcissist in a relationship with this girl or that one and even though, intellectually, I knew that he would never change, I would stick myself in my ex's phantom honeymoon phase with another girl like a punching bag in a boxing ring and then I'd beat myself up.

Yes, rumination – or the spinning of our very vulnerable mindset – can keep us "entertained" for hours, days, months and beyond…but you and I both know it is never for the better good.

We don't have to sit with our thoughts and "take it" while we're waiting for our heart to catch up with our head. Although I don't believe for a minute that we can control the thoughts as they come in, there are some things we do have control over and one would be the amount of energy we feed these thoughts as they pop in. Like anything else in this world, if we don't feed a thought, it will die. This is what we want. While we can't control our thoughts, we have all the power in the world to control our reactions to it on a case by case basis. For most of our relationship with a narcissist, we are reacting and most of this reacting is knee-jerk. To recover, all of this must stop. If you think about it, when the narcissist isn't around to poke us or push our buttons or stick knives in our backs, we truly have no excuse to be upset...not really. Back in the day, I hadn't grasped this yet and I would lie in my bed, staring at the ceiling, thinking so hard that I thought my heart would explode. If someone had been standing in my doorway watching me, they surely would have asked, "What on earth are you thinking about that is making you so upset?" And since no one ever seemed to understand my heart back then, how would I explain it?

You see, rumination is about mere thoughts and thoughts are not concrete. Thoughts can only affect us if we allow it and why would we allow something that is not concrete to cripple us? In most cases, we wouldn't because it's a waste of time to fret over something that hasn't even happened. But post break-up with a narcissist is all about wasting our own time. We will find ourselves obsessing over the same thought until we believe it has happened or will happen soon or is happening now. For example, we ruminate about the narcissist being with someone else and this makes us so insane that it actually hurts. I had to figure out a way to stop this.

When it comes time to vacate the rabbit hole, many resist because complacency has become the norm. It becomes so much easier to look the other way just one more time. For the most part, I knew that I was not the problem and so I stayed 13-years trying to convince him of that! I wanted him to "get it". Obviously, he didn't. In my quest to be right, I sacrificed my happiness. My problem, obviously, was all about boundaries. Strong and confident (something a narcissist will hatefully find attractive), I was continually booted out of the rabbit hole on my ass not long after getting invited in. However, no sooner did I hit the fresh air, I'd be kicking down the door, determined to righteously plead my case. I was determined to make him understand that HE was the asshole and that I was far from the enemy. One day, after subjecting me to a five day silent treatment, he finally flung open the door and yelled, "YOU will NOT be IGNORED!!" I replied, "Fuck NO! You're right about that!"…and so the game continued as it had done a hundred times before. I may have had self-worth but I certainly had no boundaries in place to protect it and this is where I made a very grave mistake.

It was the fact that I escaped the madness with my self-worth in- tact that compelled me to want to help others back in the boat. In doing this, though, I discovered that anyone who escapes these types of relationships with even an iota of confidence is one of the very few. Consequently, my choice to become a coach for narcissist abuse recovery (NAR) has been very humbling. What narcissists have succeeded in doing to people all over the planet is to strip away any semblance of who these people once were. Both women and men will tell me that they have ceased to even recognize themselves and to this, I *do* relate. However, the depth at which this is happening appears to be endless and it is heartbreaking. I don't have all the answers!

If you are, in this moment, feeling such desperation, I want you to listen to me and listen to me good: *YOU are not the problem. You are perfect just as you are. Do not ever base your self-worth on whether or not another person chooses to be with you. One should have nothing to do with the other.*

The very reason that a narcissist chooses you as a target is *because* you are a good person. You are everything that he/she is not and you must understand this. Nothing you could have done would have changed a thing and in due time history will repeat itself in the narcissist's new relationship. This isn't my opinion…it is fact. Of course, following his/her Instagram and Facebook posts won't confirm this for you because that is not what social media is about. Social media, under the guise of "making connections", is *set up* to create conflict within relationships of all types. Think about it. There was a time where we could simply go to our

Facebook settings and block people and be done with it. Now, if you attempt to block someone, a window pops up asking something like "Are you SURE you want to block so-and-so? Wouldn't you rather send *one more message* to see if you can work it out?" I remember seeing this message and thinking, "Facebook doesn't even care WHY I'm blocking!" The intention of Facebook, at that point, is to create doubt while at the same time *guilting* us into procrastinating on the block. When we make a conscious decision to stop looking at the narcissist's and/or the new target's social media, we are setting ourselves free in a very big way. Your self-worth is not based on Facebook or Instagram posts!

At any time, if we are struggling with a break-up and feeling inadequate because of it, we are technically basing our self-worth on the *bad behaviors* of another person. At the very least, we are basing our self-worth on the *opinion* of someone else and this is not good. Since all partners of narcissists, in my experience, are amazingly smart people (another reason we are targeted), I have to assume that, deep down, we really do understand that gauging our self-worth in this manner is illogical. How can we feel "unworthy" when the very source for this feeling is the *poster child* for unworthiness? Even knowing that this person is awful, we wonder what we could have done to make him or her happier. There is nothing logical about this. If you want to recover self-worth and self-esteem, you must practice viewing the situation from a logical perspective. Set aside the emotion and see it clearly. You were a wonderful person when you met the narcissist and you are that *same* person at the break-up. If you allow enough time for the fog to clear, this truth will be revealed to you.

Chapter: X:
The No-Contact Rule

Going "No Contact" (NC) is all about *you*. NC will ultimately give you back the clarity of mind that you lost throughout the nightmare of a relationship with a narcissist. NC will give you back the much-needed control over your life that the N worked so hard to strip away. It will give you the elusive "closure" that you continually found yourself seeking during silent treatments…when he (or she) walked out the door and literally fell off the grid, never to return. It will give you not only peace and also the peaceful *silence* that comes with a normal life. NC will provide you with an overall clarity about everything and it will allow you to see the relationship – and the narcissist - for exactly what IT is. NC *instantly* ends the vicious cycle of abuse and allows you to establish boundaries that will ultimately prevent the nightmare from ever happening again. The list of rewards goes on and on. When the person we love (who doesn't love us back) is a narcissist, nothing less than *good* can come from going No

Contact.

People may get confused but going NC is more about restoring your sanity than it is about leaving the narcissist. Nothing about the ending of this relationship is normal and therefore nothing that you've ever been feeling – and nothing that you feel right now – is normal and NC can fix this. In order to move on...in order to actually be able to enjoy the life that you deserve...you must mentally fix the damage that the narcissist has created. The only way to do this is to completely cut off any and all avenues of communication with the N once and for all – and this is what going "no contact" is all about.

In the next chapter, I'll provide you the details of the no contact process but right now I simply want you to focus on what this rule really means and why it is the key to your sanity. Knowing what we know about the narcissist's behaviors and given the spectacle of your suffering, you have to understand that, to the N, the game just never gets old. Implementing NC and sticking to it is the *only* chance you will ever have to actually put distance between yourself and the relationship. Without distance, there is no hope of recovery. Without distance, there is no hope of you ever getting over the hurt. Without distance, there is no true potential of you ever maybe meeting someone (in the future) who will love you in the way you deserve to be loved. As long as you stay in close proximity – mentally, physically or both - to the narcissist, you simply won't allow it.

Vacancy In the Rabbit Hole

I remember all too well the feeling of being completely torn apart emotionally about going no contact. For one thing, as soon as my ex even suspected that I had a plan, he'd immediately begin saying what I needed to hear. Like most narcissists, he appeared to have the uncanny ability to sense when I was getting my power back. I mean, he could push a silent treatment to the absolute limit…to a point where he knew, without a doubt, that I had passed both the anger and sadness phases and had moved into the power phase. This power phase, in essence, meant that I was moving out of my pain and into normalcy and he'd have none of that! Even as I started to feel better, I'd have a deepening anxiety that he was going to show up and ruin the whole damn thing. I knew that despite my feeling better, it was still too early to commit to never taking him back. So, during this time, I would also hope and pray that wherever he was, he'd stay there long enough for me to fully regain my footing…but that rarely happened. I'd be feeling good slightly longer than a day and – BANG – here he'd come, tapping at the door with that familiar "three-tap, pause, three-tap" knock, triggering a relationship reset. A narcissist can *sense* when an ex is feeling stronger and, when this happens, he'll quickly rearrange his current situation so that he can reappear in some way to shake things up. Don't ask me how they do it…all I know is that they can and *will* do this almost every time. No Contact, if implemented properly and with all boundaries in place, will fix much of the problem of this perfectly timed return.

From: Miriam

I left a narcissistic partner behind last year. He had given me the last silent treatment in September and when he tried to contact me in October, I had blocked his number on my mobile. He never called again. I found him on a dating website mid-December describing himself as, I kid you not, God's Gift to Women. He described himself as polite, respectful, and sensitive. In reality, the guy is a nightmare. He had told me numerous times that he wanted to spend the rest of his life with me. At the same time, he could not seem to commit. It was very confusing. I felt so abused emotionally and mentally that I had finally had enough – or so I thought. In the five years we were together, I was never invited to his house, never taken out for a meal, and never introduced to his kids. The entire relationship was manipulated to keep me on as private narcissistic supply.

I was charmed and brainwashed into believing a lie and I am pissed. I am in now therapy every week to repair the damage he inflicted while he continues on in cyber land seeking new partners. I alerted the website and gave them a quick description of what he did to me but I am sure they have not acted upon it. As of today, he was still on there, adding new pictures. I will never forgive him and thank you for telling us that it's okay to feel that. I spend most days going over the scenarios that stand out and trying to get better. I do not wish to see him ever again and need to forget he exists. Still, for some reason, he is in my head. I think it is loneliness but I am not sure. I still cannot believe the five years I spent catering to his every whim accounted to NOTHING. Now, I have nothing left but the pain.

From: Caitlyn

I've been reading your posts for a few weeks and it was as if you were writing about me. I was involved with my guy for over 3 years and it is over now and has been for some time. Like you, this was someone I had actually known through the years. We went to high school together. We were not friends, but we knew each other.

I started counseling almost a year ago. I had a feeling deep down that something wasn't quite right. Even then, knowing it was wrong for, I felt as if he had a strange power over me, almost a spell. From your writing, I know you know what I'm talking about.

I knew I needed help to find my way out even if this feeling went against my heart. I'm not sure if I qualify as going no contact because I do look his social media and still have access to his emails. He blocked me on Facebook but I do hear some of what he is doing. Your article about FB was dead on; he has blocked me at least 4 or 5 times on during the past 3 years. Yes, I have definitely felt that certain things he did in the past were intended to hurt me. Nothing more, nothing less.

I remember more than once, during these years, of having this horrible feeling that he was evil. And yet, I would still go back for more. I've never had that feeling in my life...that someone I knew and cared for truly had intent to hurt me...that it was purposeful.

Together, we have many mutual friends. It's hard because I feel that this small group of people – even those who know all the details – have a hard time acknowledging the word 'narcissist'. It's hard for anyone to accept that things were very purposeful, targeted, and planned. They believe that he is just a selfish jerk. I feel like people think I'm crazy and don't get what the big deal is.

Why this is so much harder for me to get over than my divorce – a divorce that was, by all appearances, worse than this? I don't get it. I'm a work in progress, I guess. Like you said, the "a-ha" moment doesn't make the pain magically disappear. In fact, the 'knowing' makes nothing easier – nothing.

From: Michelle

Zari, it has been a year since I posted. Healing does occur but it is very slow and takes many baby steps. However, it does get better. NC helped for me as well as a counselor who I met who happened to lead a class about narcissistic abuse. From there I met other women that also had relationships with a narc. There are so many!

For a full year, I was marking the anniversaries: one year since we met, one year since we rode our bikes, one year since he'd met another girl and was communicating with her via FB, one year since our trip and the big argument where he begged me to "just trust" him, one year since the birthday he ruined and on and on.

Then, finally, it came to the one year mark from when we had broken up. From there, I no longer felt the desire to mark the anniversaries.

However, an incident at the one year from our 1st date made me uneasy. I was feeling strong and moving forward, and then I received an email that had the look of spam, except in the address line were other women I was familiar with that had come after me. All it said was 'how are you?' plus his name. I ignored it but it did throw me off my confidence mode. After a few days, I felt better. Then, at the one year of our break up, I received the same "how are you" email and I sent it to my counselor. Some coincidence? Probably not. I didn't reply. I'd long ago blocked his cell number and blocked him from FB. We had 1 mutual FB friend and I'd had a conversation with her that something didn't seem right, but I couldn't figure out what it was. I pray a lot that she and her husband will know in the end that the narc is unhealthy.

A few weeks ago a girl in his FB group posted a photo of him from the night we'd all attended a wedding reception. I looked intensely at his eyes and noticed how dark, menacing, and arrogant he looked. Again, this threw me off for a few days. Last week, I scrolled too far down her FB page and saw the photo again. This time, instead of looking back with memories, the voice in my head shouted, "What was I thinking!"

Be gentle with yourselves out there and know that getting your strength back is your defense. Stay on the path to recovery. It's hard not to google him or look at photos and FB posts but you WILL get stronger each time you resist. We are human and we fall but we can get right back up. No one is judging us anymore. Without this person, we are free.

Zari, I continue to read your blog and posts to remind myself. Thank you. Your reach and advocacy is farther than you know.

From: Me

Hi Michelle, I placed an "Important Post" notation above your comment because I believe everyone needs to read it. I'm really proud of you for coming this far...of remaining free! I understand so well how one little blurb from the narc can knock us off the wagon but as long as we get back on and keep riding, we're good! You are doing so well...let nothing stand in your way. Keep writing and reading and sharing your wisdom. I feel that the more we pay our recovery forward, the more momentum we gain from a very understanding Universe. We have a right to be happy. We have the right to be free.

The biggest reward of NC is silence although, initially, this is hard to understand. It feels exactly like a silent treatment all over again...and who wants *that*? To this pushback, my standard response is to **change your perspective.** It only feels like a silent treatment because you perceive it that way. Once the avenues of communication are blocked to the best of your ability, it becomes *very* clear *very* quickly why NC works. Suddenly you're not worrying about or waiting on the next text or phone call because he can't do either. It won't take you long to realize that, "Hey, guess what? I can do whatever I want without the worry of being punished or manipulated!"

So, what does "No-Contact" mean? No Contact means exactly that...no contact. By definition, it's no simpler or more complicated than that. No matter where you look on the internet, no matter how many books you read on the subject, no matter who you go to for advice about narcissist abuse, you'll never get a different definition for what we all refer to as The No Contact Rule. Therefore, the list I provide is simple and concise and should serve as a refresher.

While there's no magic answer for going NC, you *will* discover that, indeed, it *is* the magic answer.

So, here you go:

1. DO block, block, block. This is the probably the most important strategy for beginning no contact because it eliminates the two most common forms of communications, the call and the text, with the text clearly being a favorite among narcissists. Narcissists love to text because it allows them to plan ahead...to really think about what words would have the greatest impact on your psyche. As codependents to this crap, we get caught up in it ourselves. Everything becomes all about a text, either the writing and sending of it or the waiting and reading and then the responding to it. To the best of your ability, make it impossible for him to call or text you. For those who still have landlines, there is always some capability for blocking numbers. Usually it's as simple as pressing the # key, a two-digit code, and then the number of the person you want to block. I can't express how important the act of blocking is to NC. It seriously breaks the mental connection.

2. DO delete, delete, delete. At the same time that you are blocking his/her number from any and all phones, you must also delete his or her name from your contact lists. This includes email, cell phone, address book and wherever you have this person's name written down.

3. DON'T visit, spy, or stalk via Social Media or Dating Sites. Going NC does *not* mean you can spy via Facebook, Instagram, or any other social media avenue. No cat-phishing or sending anonymous messages or soliciting a friend to bring you updates. Convincing someone to stay away from social media is the most difficult part of recovery when I speak with clients. Inevitably, everyone looks and then obsesses and no one ever feels better or finds any closure. You cannot get even with a narc because a narc's revenge on your revenge will always be worse. Only by pro-actively avoiding all things having anything at all to do with him can we finally begin to break the mental connection that keeps us addicted to the bullshit.

4. DON'T attempt to contact or spy via proxy. To contact or spy via proxy simply refers to the sending of any message or the harvesting of any information via human messenger. In other words, if you're feeling angry about the whole thing one night and decide to send a verbal "fuck you" message to the N via a mutual guy or girlfriend, this is breaking No Contact. *Tell James he's still an asshole for me when you see him, okay?* The same goes for scribbling a letter and having someone else drop it in the mailbox, hand deliver it, or stick it on his car. The same goes for spending time with friends that you both know and deliberately dominating the conversation with your feelings about *him* so that the word gets back sometime in the near future. Just because you didn't come right out and *ask* for someone to relay a message, if you do this with the intention of it getting back (as it most likely would), your guilty of breaking this rule. Don't do it.

So many readers that have written to me will try to use "the mutual friend" excuse as somewhat of a reason why NC will never work. What they are actually doing is trying to justify leaving the door slightly ajar for running into or having to communicate or relay a message with the narcissist in the near future. It just doesn't make sense and I refuse to see this as a viable reason for ruining the rest of your life. That being said, this particular aspect of the NC rule can get quite complicated, so I get it. The fact of the matter is that continuing to nurture or engage in relationships with friends that are also *his* friends does nothing more than keep the game going. I will discuss this again in the next chapter.

5. DON'T phone calls or emails. AND ABSOLUTELY NO TEXTING OF ANY KIND VIA ONLINE TEXT SERVICES SUCH AS PINGER AND OTHERS. Sure, we all no that there are free online texting services where you can send a text anonymously and/or from a completely different phone number. I had a blast with this brand new trolling system back in the day, believe me. I've been there, done that. However, narcs aren't stupid. He or she will know it's from you and – POOF! – the control you've enjoyed evaporates. This defeats the entire purpose of No Contact and of you having finally taken back control over your own destiny.

6. No sex, no kissing, no hugging, no shaking hands, no nothing!!! Typically, by the time we're certain its over, it's because we know that the relationship is pretty much a farce. We know that the sex, even if it's good, means absolutely nothing to the N because he can climb right out of bed and vanish with no problem. This being true, to think it's okay to touch this guy in any way after you've gone No Contact is ridiculous and defeats the entire purpose of the mission.

Now, if at any point during NC, you find yourself close enough to the narcissist to shake his hand, you've obviously already crossed the line. However, it's not a reason to give up. Many who make that first mistake view the next step as climbing all in. (*Oh why the hell not…I've already messed `up just by seeing him*). I'm here to tell you that it doesn't have to be that way. You *can* come to your senses and climb back on the NC wagon instantly. The main thing to be aware of is your intention because intention, in this situation and all others, is everything. The older I get, the clear this has become to me. With our intention in constant check, life can be nothing but authentic to the core.

And this is what we want. So, let's discuss that...

Chapter XI:
What's Your Intention?

The difference between No Contact and a Silent Treatment is the intention of the outcome - and no one knows this better than a narcissistic partner.

About four years ago, out of the clear blue and smack dab in the middle of my narcissistic nightmare, I got real strong and went No Contact on my ex before he had a chance to go silent on me. It was highly unusual behavior on my part and a shocker to both of us since it was he who typically called the communication shots. And I was able to hold on tight for quite a few weeks until his incessant pounding on my apartment door caused me to open it, letting the evil in once again for another round.

Now, at some point before I gave in, I had scribbled the words "No Contact" on the dry erase board that hung on the wall behind my desk as a reminder or affirmation, I suppose, of my own intention. After all, *this* time, I was the one going silent. But, for whatever reason, after I let the demon back in, I neglected to erase this reminder, deliberately and perhaps purposely, opening myself up to ridicule and arguments as to my reasons for breaking up. For several weeks, there I sat and there he sat and there sat those words – *No Contact* – looming on the wall behind me like the elephant in the room and neither of us said a word.

Then, one day, I happened to turn around to write a date on the board and noticed that the narcissist had made a change when I wasn't looking to my scribbled 'affirmation'. With a black marker, he had drawn an angled line through the word *No* in *No Contact* and written '*Mo*' above it so that it now read *Mo Contact* (as in slang for MORE Contact, of course). I have to admit, I thought it was pretty funny then and I think it's pretty funny even now. I left that "correction" up on that dry erase board for months after that and, again, it loomed behind me and we never said a word.

How can we possibly expect the narcissist take No Contact seriously if we don't take it seriously enough to stick to it? We can't. To a narcissist, there's absolutely no difference between a silent treatment and a little dose of no contact and, hell, he knows *all about* the dynamics of a silent treatment. Specifically, he knows that a silent treatment doesn't last forever and, therefore, the same rule must apply to the No Contact Rule. This is how he thinks when we don't show him differently...when we don't mean what we say and say what we mean.

Vacancy In the Rabbit Hole

From Karen:

Well...I've been going around in circles in my head after reading "When Love is a Lie" yesterday. I could relate to so much in the book...the silent treatments, the behavior that makes me feel like I'm going crazy even though I know I'm not, etc. But I still have this nagging little doubt in my brain telling me that I'm overreacting and maybe I'm just misunderstanding him. I'm finding it hard to believe that he's not a narcissist after reading about the holidays, though. How last Christmas he bought me a candle holder even though I bought him nice presents (he didn't even get me a candle to burn! Ha-ha). He said he would take me away for a weekend for my Christmas present and when the weekend came said he didn't have the money. Or how in February for my birthday he got me a cake...and I was shocked! As we ate it at 7PM his sons asked "why are we having cake?" And he replied "Oh it's just Krista's birthday." Or how the first time he broke up with me was the week before Easter when he was supposed to come meet my family. And how he begged me back by telling me every single thing I needed to hear this Labor Day Weekend. And then promptly disappeared 3 days before this Thanksgiving telling me that he just needed space until the weekend and then we could get together because he was stressed. Haven't seen him since. He occasionally calls or sends a nice text and says that he's stressed about his sons and doesn't have time for me right now but wants me to wait for when he's ready. I can't do this anymore. I feel like I'm going crazy! No Contact starts today! Enough is enough. This has been the worst holiday season I have EVER had.

Hi Karen:

Honestly, girl, the signs are all there. This guy is a narcissist and he's never going to stop his crap until YOU end it. The reason he sends a text every so often is only to ensure that you never get a chance to move on....to keep you in the queue in case his current fling doesn't pan out. And, believe me, a narcissist is NEVER alone although they try to make you think that so that you hang in there, waiting indefinitely for them to return. Narcissists are master jugglers...so much so that YEARS can go by without one girl ever finding out about the other or even being able to find concrete evidence. You are NOT overreacting and should NOT continue to think that. The fact is that narcissists condition us to FORGET WHAT "NORMAL" IS. It simply is NOT normal for anybody to behave that way, to neglect you and avoid you and break promises and plans. You shouldn't be willing to accept that anymore under any circumstances. If you do, you will waste so much of your precious time. Life is too short for that, girlfriend.

Block him. Make it so he can not communicate with you under any circumstance. It is the only way. Otherwise, the game is going to repeat itself like a broken record for as long as he can get away with it. And if he comes back, you can bet that someone ELSE is getting the silent treatment. And around and around it will go.

What we allow will continue.

Most narcissist victims, even as painful as it is, *do* understand that implementing No Contact is and always will be the only effective means to gaining back our sanity. So, we spend a lot of time talking about it and trying to create new and better ways to maintain it so that we don't do exactly what the narcissist thinks we're going to do - give in. Be true to your intention because there is no reason to lie. You are either in it or you are not. Silent treatments, as we know, are temporary. An unexpected, unnecessary silent treatment – aside from being cruel and unusual and the narcissist's favorite "punishment" - is intended to prove a point or to teach a lesson or to buy time to cheat or whatever he or she has in mind. The intention of No Contact should be nothing other than to end it. Sure, it would be nice if No Contact hurt the narcissist in the same way that his or her silence hurts us but this never happens. Narcissistic injury is not the same as the gut-wrenching feeling we get when we're discarded. It's not even close. Going NC actually gives us the last word – finally. NC, whether we know it or not, is the closure from the narcissist that we've been looking for.

I was very guilty of not taking the No Contact rules seriously (as shown in my *Mo Contact* anecdote). I was guilty of going in (or out) with the wrong intention. I'm certain that I went "no contact" more than once to get the narcissist's attention. This is wrong. We can't seriously implement No Contact yet still look at/allow texts, emails, Facebook contact, or continue to drive-by, etc. If the intention is really to end it, then all of that must stop. Numbers must be blocked or changed, emails deleted, Facebook accounts blocked or, better yet, deactivated. We can't have it both ways.

From Janice:

My relationship with the Narc started exactly a year ago. I was in another state for a new job and living with an ex when we met online. We would talk and text for hours and he was like an angel from the heavens. Finally, I had met a man who could actually hear and understand me. Then, he asked to see me in person and, after some discussion, I agreed to meet him for a dinner. It was like love at first sight. He was Mr. Perfect and we started to see each other more often. Mostly, I was driving to see him.

One day, during a visit, he tells me he cannot stand that I am living with my ex and that I should come live with him. My ex wasn't a bad guy, he was actually very nice, but the relationship was over. So... after his offer, he drove me back to the state where I live and on that same day, I resigned from my job giving one week notice and left my house, taking just my clothes and without saying anything to my ex. I was so in love. He spoke of getting married and having a baby and a beautiful house. I wouldn't have to work, he said, because he had a really good job. He said I could go for my dream of getting my PhD without worrying how I could afford it.

For the first month, it was like a romance in the movies. After that, he stared checking my phones, criticizing my friends and my relationships with them and he also deleted some of my friends from my phone. Since I had moved to another state, I didn't know anybody and the only way I could socialize was with my friends over the phone. He began creating nonsense arguments that made me feel desperate to defend myself and he was making a fuss over nothing. Each argument was stronger than the one before and I started crying as if I was having a nervous breakdown. Suddenly, it was as if this man did not hear me and there was no logic to what he was saying or doing. But at the end, he would always hug me and say he loved me and that I was the love of his life.

I began to think about his jealousy and figured I could simply fix it later. He bought a new house right before we met that contained no furniture to even sit on and he told me I could buy what I wanted. He said that he wanted our families to meet and they did. My parents start making wedding plans. We flew to his parents and they threw an engagement party. We stayed for two weeks and during that time, the mother bitched that she had no time alone with him and asked why I had to stay for so long. He said he would be so bored without me if I left.

After this vacation, strange things started to happen. He said he wanted to break up, he was not happy with me and would be better off without me. After all these ceremonies and parties, I couldn't figure out why until I saw a 10 page nasty email from his mother about me and my family. She called me a gold digger, saying I was worse than his ex-wife who took everything from him when she was leaving and so on. I couldn't believe my eyes and talked to him about it. He said it was nonsense and him wanting to break up had nothing to do with her email. We were just fighting too much....Because of me? OR because of his non-logical arguments over anything?

Now, it had been two months since I moved in and he went back and forth between wanting me to leave and wanting me to stay. I couldn't leave because I had loaned him my entire savings when he asked to buy a car and I had no money. When I asked for my money back, he told me to count it as rent for the months that I lived in his house, our travels and the furniture we bought for his home. Really? 10K ? By now, I had found a job in the same city but I couldn't cope with the depression and insomnia. I even thought about killing myself. I started taking two antidepressants as the psychiatrist told me that I was in major depression but the side effects of the medications made it all worse.

Today, he claims to still be in a financial crisis and cannot pay me back. I am in the situation now where I have to live far from where I used to live and I literally know nobody. I am still living in this house with him with no support for my anguished mental state that he created. He keeps telling me he will give me my money in a week or a month... but he does not. Even if he does, I don't know how to start a new life all by myself after all the romance and *promises and disappointments... I am 37 years old, never married and I have no hope for the future now.*

From: me

Hi Janice,

Your story is so sad and so awful and he is a horrible man but you are so young, sister. Of course it was the email that caused this mama's boy to change his mind and this makes him an absolute COWARD. Is it at all possible to go back to the state that you came from to stay with one of your friends? Can you call your old job? Can you stay with family? How about your ex? I truly feel that THIS GUY was the gold digger who saw a wonderful girl with a little bit of money he could steal from. Is your name on anything because, yes, he does absolutely owe you that money but I doubt you will ever see it. Your mental health is more important at this point...God! What a complete narcissistic fool. Janice, you DO know how to start a new life all by yourself...you just do it as you did before but do it in a place that is familiar. You are only 37!! Save your money...in fact, HOARD it and give him nothing. In the meantime, call the people from your old life and make a plan. You made a mistake...so what...so many of us have done it. You must have a friend from your old life that you can trust. I really care and want to know how you are doing, my sad sister.....Stay strong and know that you can have a wonderful long life with a bright future...you really can!

The feelings that compel us to break no contact can be controlled and we have to understand this throughout recovery. The narcissist relies on the fact that an *empath* is ruled by his or her emotions so he or she will wait patiently for the fallout. When I realized that my reactions were completely under my control, my world instantly changed. No matter what he did and no matter *how I felt*, I didn't have to react in ways that kept me on the hook for future letdowns. In these types of relationships, because everything that occurs is so out of the norm, we can easily spin out of control. It doesn't have to be that way.

In recovery, we have to practice a healing strategy that involves three elements: **persistence, patience,** and the process of being **pro-active**. And part of this plan is to understand and recognize the dangers of certain daily triggers that could cause a backslide. So, let's have a look…

Chapter XII:
Avoiding Triggers

Once we've gone No Contact, avoiding the triggers that can cause us to backslide becomes all-important. For each of us, while some triggers will be unique to the relationship, most of the triggers will be exactly the same. Hence, the reason for the list provided in this section. I consider the list to be a one-size-fits-all simply because relationships involving narcissists are often interchangeable.

What makes the triggers after No Contact so intense is that they actually signify that we are in control – and this isn't a normal feeling. We suddenly have to make decisions about how to handle the triggers because we initiated the break-up. During a silent treatment, the narcissist is in control until we turn it around. Up to that point, we feel powerless. Even if we fight for control periodically and achieve it, it never lasts. Moreover, we learn that giving up control to the narc is the easiest way to make peace, so we just do it. Also, when we're *not* in control in our relationship, the sexual tension is at its highest and we cherish this because sex is often the *only* connection that we have to this person. Yes, we are certainly willing to give up control for some good sex and a few crumbs of attention. Sad, but true.

So, committing to NC puts us in a vulnerable place and the triggers are everywhere like boulders on the highway. If we don't pay attention, one trigger can be the cause for disaster. Within seconds, we're back to the start line, power dialing his or her phone and apologizing for things we didn't even do. I'm telling you this so you can be aware and ready for battle. Get your avenues of support in order so that you can deflect and intercept the punches. Allow no room for incoming pain. In fact, whenever you recognize a trigger, yell "Incoming!" and take cover, run, or drive off. You can do this.

Below are just a handful of the universal triggers that can send us scrambling back into the rabbit hole. Take mental notes, remember, and recognize.

1. **You need "closure".**

    The truth is...*no, you don't*. Closure is a made-up word invented by narcissists to keep exes in the loop, searching for something they will never find. In real life, closure means nothing. It exists in the movies when the problem of the main character is tied up and resolved in a nice pretty package. That bittersweet feeling of "understanding and acceptance" is what we *imagine* that we're missing during a silent treatment or after a discard. The truth, if we were being honest, is that finding closure is more about having the last word or getting revenge or "exposing". "Closure" just sounds better.

All that being said, when the need for "closure" arises, recognize it first and then dismiss it. This is *no contact* and your "lack of" closure shouldn't matter. The fact that you've gone No Contact *is* your closure and it is also the *last word* (by being no word at all!). Going NC immediately puts you in the driver's seat, allowing you to take control, finally, of your own life.

2. **You miss the sex.**

I understand this very well because sex was the *only thing* I ever really missed when my relationship was over. However, just like everything we did together, I was the only one who put meaning to it. Narcissists do not feel "love" and connection as normal people do and therefore the sex he or she has is given little value. Sure, you both enjoyed it and perhaps this was the only time that you felt he or she really cared about you. But the connection, as we know, is completely one-sided. Consistently great sex with a narc even for years will not keep the narcissist from cheating or thinking about cheating. So, what are you really missing?

Don't allow "body" emotions to get in the way of your logical thinking. During NC, do not entertain the idea of a booty call because it will negate your intention. Believe me, the pain you feel now will only intensify and you will be right back where you started.

3. **You forgot to tell him something**.

No, you didn't. There isn't a single thing you need to tell him (or her) that he or she deserves to hear. Let it go.

4. **Everything reminds you of him**.

In retrospect, this makes me laugh and I'll tell you why. When I was separated from the narcissist, everything and anything – *no matter what it was* – made me feel those butterflies. So, when I took a good look…asking myself, "Okay, what does this remind you of?", my *truthful* answer was that everything reminded me of what he *wasn't* or what he *didn't* do that I always wanted. Whatever I saw, whatever song came on the radio, the smell in the air…*whatever it was*…was only reminding me of *what we could have had but didn't*. To deflect this type of trigger, see it for what it *really* is…confirmation that NC is the way to go. Even the good times with a narc inevitably end in radioactive fallout. Why cry about it?

There is a painful truth behind every trigger. The trigger is showing us what was fake or what we never ever had. *This is why triggers make us cry.* Learn to recognize the reality. In the meantime, avoid that which makes you weep for no reason. Turn off the radio. Take down the pictures. Take a detour past your "favorite" restaurant. Stop crying over objects or mere thoughts. NC is about saving your life.

5. **He still has his stuff at your house**.

Of course, he does. Narcissists love to leave trinkets behind as painful memories. This is an age-old ploy and we will even do it in reverse, leaving stuff at the narcs house for *almost* the same reasons (#6). It's a recognizable game that needs no explanation. Pack up his shit and send it UPS. Resist the urge to send him an angry text telling him to come and get his things. Feel free to throw it all out or even sell it. The narcissist doesn't care about his stuff anymore than he cares about you. That's why he leaves bits of it everywhere that he goes. You know this. Enough said.

6. **You still have stuff at his house**.

By leaving stuff at the narc's place, we mark our territory. If we leave *enough* stuff, it might even look like we *live* there. But, as we know, none of this matters. If we have to leave trinkets behind just to have a reason to reconnect, this is clearly not a sustainable relationship, right? So, if you must, have a friend that you trust collect it for you or, better yet, consider the items a loss and let it go. If you know in advance that you are planning NC, casually take the items home beforehand.

7. You need a ride or have a flat tire.

Call a friend. Better yet, get AAA Roadside Service. Chances are you couldn't count on the narc when you *were* together. And, whatever you do, please do not *create* emergencies as an excuse to call or text him. Be aware and *beware* of this trigger because it can happen in a split second. The littlest thing can become an "emergency".

8. He owes you money.

There's nothing worse than feeling that both your heart and bank account have been broken. However, my feeling on this is that unless it's a ridiculous amount of money, he or she's a millionaire, or you have a lawyer and the energy to go to court (which *has* worked), then it's time to cut the financial ties. This also means *no using the money* as an excuse for contact down the road as it would only defeat your purpose.

9. **A friend calls to tell you that she saw the N on Facebook bragging about a new girl.**

First of all, this particular person is *not* your friend and mutual friends should be off limits. You have to make it clear at the beginning of NC that you wish *not* to talk about the narcissist or be privy to updates. Those that are true friends will abide by your wishes and find other things to talk about. Those that aren't will quickly show their true colors and can always be added to the No Contact list.

10. **You drank too much.**

Avoid dealing with your pain with drugs and alcohol. It simply never works. While a night out with the girls or guys might *sound* like a steam-releaser, we both know exactly what happens after a few drinks. You become a drunk-dialing fool and all your NC efforts will be for naught. For at least the first few months, avoid this from happening by avoiding the bar completely.

11. **You had sex with someone else and now you *really* miss him.**

I tried this several times over thirteen years and I discuss it at length in both of my books. When we're younger, rebound sex is an easy way to get over an ex. But then the years pass and something in us changes. As I got older (and became more attached to the sexual aspect of my relationship with the N), the harder it became to duplicate that same feeling with someone else. Post-narc rebounds sent me spiraling backwards. I actually took on the narc's qualities, disappearing after a fun overnight date and ghosting the guy completely. I left a few really nice guys wondering what the hell happened. It was wrong of me to do that, it really was, but all I could think about at sunrise was finding my way back to my ex.

The ties we have to the narcissist run deep and in order to recover, we simply have to put distance between ourselves and any type of physical relationship. This is very, very important and it's not forever. The wait, I promise, will be worth it.

What about mutual friends & family ties?

Mutual friends can be a backsliding trigger and also our imaginary ties to the narcissist's family. Both are easily avoided if we cut the ties that bind. Once we end it or choose never to go back, we often feel that we owe certain people an explanation. Trust me, we do not. In fact, I suggest that you say absolutely *nothing* to anyone. The word will get out in the manner that words *always* get out and you shouldn't have to say a thing. The intention here is to become disconnected from the suffering.

Relevant to mutual friends, this will have to be your call. How important to you are these mutual friends? In my case, it appeared that whoever happened stop by after the break-up had nothing to talk to me about *but* the break-up or about what my ex was doing. Sometimes they would choose to tell me things about him that I never knew, things he had been doing all along, and I thought it strange that they hadn't told me that before. Mutual friends simply do not work. Just looking into the eyes of someone who I knew might be looking into *his* eyes later made me very anxious. I suddenly became very disinterested in the company of certain people and I felt okay about it. In other cases, I found that I could step back just far enough to not always be available for conversation and this was okay too. We simply must break the ties that bind in order to be free. Those who sincerely care about you will understand and be there for you whenever you're ready. A chosen few will automatically know that speaking non-stop about your ex or inadvertently slipping in an update is a no-no. Having seen enough of your pain and anguish in the past, friends will abide by your wishes. And if they don't, it's okay because they weren't your friends to begin with.

The same rules apply to family members of the narcissist whom you may have felt close to. This is slightly out of the norm since most victims are kept separated from the narcissist's family by the narcissist him or herself for obvious reasons. After all, keeping you close to the family might mean that you're *like* family and we know *that's* not true. Since my ex would move to his mother's house with almost every disappearance, he made sure that I felt unwelcome there. During silent treatments, as much as I wanted to pound on his mother's door, I never did. Yes, cat-like strolls through the cul-de-sac were about as close as I ever got to that house after the third or fourth year. Later, when it was finally over, I was grateful for this conditioning.

The truth of the matter is that, to members of the family, the narcissist is still blood and you're not. Let family members go and you'll be glad that you did. You will feel an even bigger sense of freedom and separation from the drama.

From Jules:

I have been with a guy for 12 years. When we met, he was supposedly single and had been out of his "relationship" for over a year. However, he and his ex were co-parenting. I found this to be quite admirable given that my ex-husband left me with 3 children under the age of 12, totally disappearing off the face of the earth. He later re-emerged, some nine years later, with a younger model in tow. Our youngest had just turned 18 years old so his comment then was, "These children are all grown adults now and not my responsibility".

So, Mr. New Guy looked pretty good. His reason for not being with his ex was that they continually argued. He felt that her full time job kept her from caring for her family and they all fended for themselves. I was also told that she was not welcome in his family. Apparently, there had been some really bad blood years prior to the birth of their son. This story was validated by his brother, his dad and other friends who I met and spent time with. From what I could see, everyone thought that we were a couple and other members of his family told me that he was single, that he had left her, and that things were not good at their home. They confirmed that he had moved out and was living on his own of which I was aware.

During our first year, he met with my children and all was good. Then, after two years, he moved in with me and one year later, he moved out. I have to say, we did break up on our own with no outside help. Then, some 5 months later, he calls, my heart does somersaults and we are back in a relationship but taking it slowly. I move, hoping he is moving with me, but a couple of work-related excuses later, he decides that he is not. In retrospect, I see that this went on year upon year upon year. Then, in May this year, for whatever reason, I decided to drive past the place where he was living and he wasn't there. On a hunch, I drove by his ex's house and lo and behold, his car was there. So, before I muster up the courage to storm in, he spots me and comes out. He tells me that we need to talk, and as I have a total meltdown in the car, we return to my house separately and he then drops the bombshell. He had moved back in with his ex some two years back!

Now, supposedly, he has hit rock bottom. We've been talking for days about this and he can't bring himself, even as he lives with HER, to say that it is over between us. Why did I not see this? He says that he is now in therapy trying to understand why he led two separate lives. And here I am, a total wreck, still giving him a chance. Is this wrong of me? Is he a narcissist and why did I not know or see the signs? We are, at present, still split as he agrees we are making each other ill. He has texted requesting time to make it right and that he will be there for me. Really? When???

From Me:

Hi Jules, at some point, what does it matter if there is a label to define him? Awful is awful. Stay away from him. You busted him red handed and this is the reason for his confession and phony attempts to rehabilitate. He won't learn a thing in therapy because that is not his intention. In my opinion, therapy, for a narc, is something to appease a lover after being caught. I hear it all the time. Why put your life on hold while he fakes his way through? He is enjoying the fact that he has "gotten away with" telling you that he has been with her for two years. You still remain true. Why do this to yourself? It will never be sustainable. He knows right from wrong...he simply doesn't care... and there is nothing redeemable about that, narcissist or not.

How to Handle the Smear Campaign

As partners of narcs, we've all been targets of a smear campaign at one time or another. After all, breaking up with a narc isn't like any other break-up or divorce we've ever had. There is going to be a radioactive fallout. Mutual friends, family, and, of course, children, can all become involved but it doesn't have to be scary. I discovered, quite by accident, that by making one amazingly simple change to my reaction, I could all but *instantly* change the dynamic of the smear itself. The key, my friends, is to say NOTHING at all…not a single world…and, believe me, there will be power in your silence.

Naturally, when someone is talking bad about us to others, our first reaction is to want to defend ourselves. In many situations, this is okay but not when the culprit is a narcissistic ex. Why? Because narcissists are fools, that's why – and when they talk smack, they *sound* like fools as well. If we stay silent after the break-up, we automatically look like the better person. This simple strategy is foolproof and will save you the trouble of *ever* having to defend yourself against the narcissistic nonsense, even in the company of mutual friends.

Whether we were together or apart, my ex was the biggest smack talker I ever knew. No matter where he was, if there were people within earshot that knew me or knew *of* me, he happily talked smack. When word got back to me, I was simply too embarrassed to respond, even in my own defense. Now, unbeknownst to my ex, I had stopped speaking of our relationship to anyone nearly two years before it finally ended. I just didn't see the point. As a result, there were people who knew of us separately who weren't even sure we were ever a couple. So, when my ex showed up around town to talk smack, people were not only surprised but concerned. Here's my ex, running his mouth about me to people I knew who, after a couple of minutes, were actually thinking, *Holy Crap, does Zari even know this guy? She's never even mentioned him!*

Seriously, he looked like a fool. A grown man whining about his ex-girlfriend to a roomful of people is nonsensical enough but to do it in a room full of people who actually *like* that girl is just ridiculous. So, in my embarrassment, I said nothing and the more he talked, the more ridiculous he looked. As time passed, even as stories were relayed to me, my anxiety about feeling 'defenseless' dwindled away. I realized that people weren't expecting me to defend myself or to lower myself to his level. Basically, they were letting me know how foolishly he was behaving. I didn't need to respond or defend and so I did not. Eventually the messengers disappeared and the smear campaign subsided. I am telling you, this works! As a narcissist should know, *silence can be very, very powerful.*

Now, all that being said, going 'no contact' with a narcissist with whom you have children is a little different. He or she will still try to control you and then validate that control even while separated and/or divorced. Children may be caught in the crossfire and smear campaigns can be brutal. But listen, the no-defense strategy can still be maintained with dignity and there are other tactics to use as well. The **no-contact, no defense rule** still stands with just a tad of modification added to make it work as a co-parent.

Chapter XIII:
The Co-Parenting Dilemma

The only thing harder than going No Contact with a narcissist is going No Contact with a narcissist who happens to be your baby daddy or momma. Based on the countless emails and comments that I receive from victims who struggle to co-parent with a narcissistic ex, it's clear to me that there are no easy solutions. In fact, up until I began to write this book, I was starting to fear that perhaps there were *no* solutions but I quickly decided that this simply wasn't acceptable. So, after giving the subject some very careful thought, I came up with a slightly different perspective on this very unique co-parenting scenario. Ultimately, I decided that co-parenting with a narcissistic ex and having a peaceful life *can* happen because it *must* and that the Agony of Defeat typically felt by the victim parent was not insurmountable.

Can a narcissist love his/her children? This is the big question, of course, and, unfortunately, the answer is no. The truth is that a narcissist can no more love his or her children than he or she can love a partner, friend, family member, or anyone else. I've never seen it happen. I've never read about it happening. I've never heard about it happening. It's just not possible. An N is an N is an N. If history could somehow prove that even the slightest possibility existed... that narcissists could, in fact, love their own children...I'd be tempted to think that narcissism perhaps was fixable. But there is no history *anywhere* that shows this...no history, that is, that is based in fact and not in wishful thinking. No, narcissists do not *and cannot* love their children any more than they can love you, the person who suffers for them the most.

Now, having said that, do not be misled into thinking that narcissists do not find their children *useful* under certain circumstances because...*oh yeah*...they most certainly do. In fact, the N who is a combination "ex-partner" and "co-parent" has the luxury of circulating, surviving, and thriving at levels of evil *far beyond* that of the typical narcissist. The narcissistic co-parent is indeed a Super Power in his or her own right! Yes, he or she who holds this coveted position is awarded the type of false entitlements that a single non-parent narcissist only *dreams* about. And for the victim partner who wants to get away, a break-up with this narcissistic superpower too often appears to be a hopeless situation. To implement No Contact on this person only guarantees a *brand new* narcissistic show of chaos that promises to be far more damaging than the first, second, and third. And, this time, it will be the children who get bumped to the top of the N's hit list.

Is it possible to go No Contact with a narcissistic co-parent? In many ways, no... at least not in the way that **No**

Contact was originally intended. Victims who want/need the torture to stop but still have to deal with co-parenting issues are left without certain 'no contact' strategies that other victims take for granted. As a victim who co-parents, how do you block a phone number, move away, refuse to answer the door, blow off the in-laws, and so forth when there are children involved? You can't. How do you flat out refuse to communicate with a parent that the children (bless their hearts) have been duped into loving? How do you deal with the fact that the narcissist talks smack about you to the kids and you can't even defend yourself (because you choose to do the right thing and stay quiet)?

Because the narc, as a parent, is not a normal human, he is, without a doubt, going to use the children as his narcissistic tactic and weapon of choice to cut you to the very bone. Since he clearly has no conscience, dragging the children into the dirt is nothing but a thing and the easiest way to hurt you. The narcissistic co-parent will use every excuse in the book pertaining to the children to intrude upon your new life. At some point, he may even try to scare you into submission - either by threatening to call CPS (for no reason at all) or by saying that he won't be bringing the children back after visitation or by saying he or she will see you in court. Granted, we never know whether or not they will follow through until they do or don't but the thought is nonetheless horrifying since you *know* he will cross all boundaries both in court and out if he thinks it is necessary.

Unfortunately, now that you've separated from this person, you will be forced to watch the nightmare that was *your* relationship played out once again and this time towards the children. It's likely the narcissistic father or mother will continually make plans with the children and then not show up or even bother to call to cancel. He will promise to call and then conveniently forget. He may even miss holidays altogether, choosing instead to be with his "new" victim family and partner. He will relish the thought that now, even with the relationship being over, he can continue to torture you by torturing the children. And since the children, at least while they're young, tend to love a narcissistic parent unconditionally no matter how neglectful and indifferent he/she may be, the N ultimately gets nearly a life time to make sure you are never happy again!

So, what is the answer? The answer, first, is to know that the relationship between you and the N is over. At this point, despite how he appears to others, you already know the type of parent that he really is and must proceed to use this information to (for once) serve your own purpose. How much time did the N really spend with the children anyway? Narcissists are historically not doting fathers and mothers or even participating fathers and mothers. Over and over, I hear stories of narcissistic fathers walking out just weeks after a child is born to start a brand new life with someone else. I hear about new mothers being subjected to silent treatments immediately after coming home from the hospital. Silent treatments!! Can you imagine that?? I hear about narcissists who've walked out just days before Christmas, leaving a family of little children with not the slightest idea where daddy went. This may not be exactly the case with your ex-N but I bet its close. Narcissists have the amazing ability to be...well...narcissists no matter what. Expect it to happen and do not fear it. There's nothing new under the sun except that he or she doesn't live with you. Use this knowledge to your advantage. You are a good person. He or she is not.

The secret to achieving some level of survivable co-parent No Contact with a narcissist is that you, too, must strive to be a Super-Power! You must develop thicker skin than you ever thought possible so that every nasty comment he throws your way rolls off your back. You must be able to take an emotional beating without anyone around you being the wiser. You must learn to *detach, detach, detach* from the nonsense and *commit, commit, commit* to setting boundaries and making rules of engagement. Communication, if possible, should be limited to text, email, and the sporadic phone call...and it must *only* concern sensible/reasonable issues about the children. And, really, how many of *those* can there be that have to involve the N? Not many.

The following three pointers are the rules of engagement that helped me through a very bitter divorce and up and over my fear of losing control of my rights as the better parent. I learned how to stand up.

The Three Rules of Co-Parenting Engagement

#1 Ten Minutes to Talk

With my son's father, I learned to use a ten-minute rule. There is absolutely nothing that can't be explained, described, announced, or stated in ten minutes. If you must, wear a watch and mentally start the clock when the phone rings or when he or she pulls up for a pick-up or drop-off. With a narcissist, the conversation will rarely be a good one so you will have plenty of opportunity to practice at perfecting this strategy. Learn to "direct" the conversation back to the kids if that's how it started. And if it didn't start that way, then you should end the conversation anyway. Give fair warning and attempt to end civilly but don't stress it. Simply hang up. Use your head. It is your decision about what is truly important enough to be talking about. Ten minutes and you're done.

#2 Detachment & Indifference

For the ten minutes of talk time, whether in person or on the phone, do not react to *anything*. Show nothing but detachment and indifference. He or she is always looking for a reaction and your job now is not to give it. This is the hardest part perhaps but it also brings the biggest reward – your sanity. If you have to beat the wall once inside or after you hang up, then so be it but I promise it won't be that bad. The purpose here is to train the narcissist – and yes, this can be covertly done – to understand that his words don't affect you like they used to. In the beginning, the more detached and indifferent you appear, the harder he will try to upset you. Don't let it happen. You are allowing only ten minutes max of conversation where topic worthiness is up to *you*. Seriously, it will become fun to deflect his emotional punches with your stone cold and logical-minded mental armor.

#3 Don't Talk Smack (About Him/Her) to the Kids

And I mean EVER. This particular rule, as difficult as it is to achieve consistently, brings the biggest reward: (eventual) *total respect from your kids.* And the great thing is that you can start *now* even if, up until this point, talking smack about the narcissist to the kids is all you've ever done. It simply doesn't matter as long as long as it stops now. You see, the great thing about children is that they really just want you to be happy. So, be happy! Believe me, three weeks of coming home to a happy parent after spending the weekend with the narcissist who did nothing but talk smack and they will be SOLD. I experienced this first hand with my son. His dad would take him out of my arms and call me a whore as he got in the car. I begged him not to do it but he didn't care. For the first year, I played into it and life was a chaotic, horrific mess, especially for my son who probably didn't feel comfortable at either house. Then, I made a conscious decision to stop reacting and I meant it. It's one of the few decisions in my life from which I can honestly say I never wavered. Even though he loved his dad, my son looked forward to coming home to a stress free house. I stopped talking smack about his dad in his presence and I never asked him questions. I did say to my son, just one time, that I was not going to talk about his daddy anymore in a bad way but if his daddy talked bad about me or asked him questions that he felt pressured into answering, that he was not to feel guilty and it was okay. And from there we went.

So, do not worry about and/or feed into the enormous amount of trash-talking going on behind your back. In fact, say nothing and simply observe, allowing the N to talk trash about mommy *all day long* if he wants to. It's just another smear campaign and the best defense is no defense at all. Sit quietly on the sidelines while the pathetic narcissist digs his own parental grave – and he *will* dig it because he just can't help himself (or herself). Take comfort in the fact that children are strong, resilient, and smart. They *will* grow up one day and see the narcissistic parent for what he/she is and *you* will come out the winner. The narc's mask always slips and that's a fact.

Vacancy In the Rabbit Hole

Understand that in staying quiet, I changed everything. My son and I bonded immensely and guess what? I *always* looked like the better parent and he remembered that as he grew up. It's not an easy thing to do – to be quiet while the smear campaign is in full force – but once you get the hang of it, the weight lifts. Again, the best defense to a smear campaign is *no defense at all.*

You must believe in your heart that no matter how hurtful the narcissist is or how evil his intention, you are still free! The relationship is *over*. You may now see the narcissist as nothing more than an annoying sperm donor and treat him accordingly. He deserves nothing less, nothing more. For *years*, the narcissist has been methodically managing down your expectations...preparing for this very day....setting the stage for *this* break-up because he *knew* it would come...it *had* to come. The narcissist co-parent counts on the fact that his passive-aggressive conditioning of your responses to his words and behaviors has stuck and that you still fear what he *could* do, *might* do, *will* do. He counts on *his* control in this situation and *your* emotional fragility. The fact that he gets to use the kids against you is just an added bonus!

Turn it around by having *no more fear*. It's time to up the ante. First, if the narcissist has a girlfriend, tell him you want to be communicative with her *about the children*. Now, the N will *hate* this but that's too bad. Normal couples in normal break-ups speak to "the others" all the time. If you show that you're willing and actually *prefer* to communicate with the OW, the N is likely to begin behaving immediately to ensure this never happens – and that's fine too (it's what we want). I'd be willing to bet that, within a short amount of time, the narcissist will begin to back out completely since the fun of making you suffer will have been taken out of the equation. Using this particular communication twist clearly sends a message to the Narcissistic co-parent that says: *I don't care about you anymore.*

Even if it hurts, do it. What you are doing here is forcing him to comply with NC unless YOU find that it is absolutely necessary to break it. You now call the shots. Do not allow fear, or your ego to keep you from being free. Do not let your emotions rule your actions. **You can *still* initiate and implement your own version of No Contact with the narcissist co-parent.** You can *still* move on with your life. Chances are high that if you show indifference, detachment, and a refusal to play The Game of Life on his terms in any way, the narcissist will do what he has always done and vanish anyway. The children will *still* grow up to be wonderful people. In the end, you, as the co-parenting ex victim, will be stronger than any of us who have embarked on this journey.
Don't allow the co-parenting dilemma to become an excuse to stay connected with the N. Know in your heart that your decision to end it with the N despite the fact that you have children together will *always* be the right decision.

Chapter XIV:
Suffering Is a Process

Mentally letting go of the narcissist is part of a recovery process that cannot be rushed. However, long after my break-up, I discovered that there are *phases* to our suffering post-break-up that we complete successfully without even knowing it. It took hundreds of conversations with clients for me to figure this out. I started to see a pattern in recovery that no one talks about…a pattern that has to do with the suffering and how we move through it. If I had been aware of this one thing at any time during my own experience, I wouldn't have continually given up so easily. I would have never begged for anything. I could have pushed aside the *compulsion* to break no-contact because I would have realized, at that point, that it wasn't the narcissist I was even missing.

Okay, so what do I mean by this? I mean that we *become* the suffering. I mean that when the final break-up with a narcissist occurs, **our sadness is actually less about our grief over the loss of the relationship than it is about the fact that we've become the suffering that was associated with it.** Read that sentence one more time. The truth is that we spend far more time with the "suffering" than we ever do with the narcissist...so it's natural to become attached to it. The sadness becomes a familiar connection that keeps us in the loop all by itself. The narcissist, of course, has understood this all along and this is why he or she likes to keep us sad and anxious. The narc's theory is that as long as we're suffering, he or she can feel fairly confident that we'll always be in the queue. For the most part, his theory is correct but we have the power to change it. At the end, we *can* get past the suffering if we only first realize that it's not at all about the narcissist. We just *think* that it is. Our grief is about our *attachment* to the suffering and sadness and there are three phases to the process of letting this all go.

So, when I hear *Why am I still so sad? I don't even want him back! What's wrong with me?,* I know that this person is recovering but this is only because I finally understand the process. The person I'm speaking with, however, is usually beside themselves with self-doubt. I explain that this particular form of cognitive dissonance is a good thing and that it's different from the cognitive dissonance that makes us doubt the narcissist is even a narcissist.

When you've reached that point of feeling crazed over the fact that you still feel sad, you've actually passed through the **first phase of suffering**. In other words, you are no longer in denial! It's during phase one that those who call me will ask, "Are you sure he's a narcissist? Are you *sure?*" (to which I typically respond, "The fact that you're calling me tells me you already know the answer to that.") Still, my client may continue to struggle or choose not to believe me. A month and a few phone calls later, when I hear "I know he's a narc and I don't even like him! Why do I still feel so devastated?", I know that this person has moved on to **phase two** and *now* the attachment she (or he) feels is only *to the sadness itself*. While this attachment can, in many ways, be more painfully bittersweet than our attachment to the narc, it's much easier to let go of...but first you must believe that it exists...that our suffering, indeed, is a process!

Which phase are YOU in?

From Jamie:

I have been No Contact for some time now and I have been educating myself for the last year on just who I was in a relationship with. I recently found your website and I have to say, I am learning so much and have had quite a few light bulb moments today after reading some of your entries. Your article about triangulation really struck a chord with me. Other sites describe triangulation as being about another person only (usually the OW). No where do they include things like "cell phones", other inanimate objects or a place as being used for triangulation. Granted, most of the triangulation I experienced occurred in passing - almost covert - and much of the time I didn't notice because I actually felt secure within myself. But now, in retrospect,

I can clearly see how many things he tried – sometimes successfully - triangulating me with: his phone, his job, other women (of course), his daughters, his vehicle, places he wanted to visit, and more. When we'd be apart, for example, he'd be sure to say he was out but he say it in such a way that I would freak out. Occasionally I'd think to myself, "What in the world?? Why am I feeling this way?" when this happened but, like you say, he'd continue to do it until I "got it". Then, when I'd blow up or call him out on a lie, he'd call me crazy, jealous, needy and too dramatic. Never in my life have I ever been called these things! After I met this parasite, this was all I ever heard! Because I couldn't explain what was happening, I thought maybe he was right. He was so covert in his abuse...so passive-aggressive...that I was always left to fill in the blanks. If I asked questions, he'd simply gas-light me until I shut-up.

This is just a drop in the bucket as to everything he did to me in just one year's time. All the pathological lying, cheating, and so much more. Anyway, it was a year ago this week when, having finally had enough, I up and discarded him before he had a chance to do it to me. It felt very empowering to be the one to leave, believe me, yet at the same time it was hard because I still loved him. He, of course, was full of narcissistic rage, sending text after text and using my kids to get to me. To watch him go from raging one minute to being sugary sweet the next, it was pure insanity. He remained incessant, hacking into my accounts, texting and emailing all hours of the day and night, etc. The anxiety of this became too hard to handle and I finally contacted my lawyer who helped me file a Stalking Injunction against him. Now, if he attempts to contact me in any way at all (even through another party), he will go to jail. Early on, he requested a hearing to get the injunction overturned but was quickly laughed out of the courtroom when I showed up with phone records and every email and text he ever sent me.

The bottom line is that I MADE him leave me alone. I MADE him unable to hoover me again and again and I forced him to respect my boundaries (or at least abide by them). Clearly, filing that injunction saved my life. I truly believe that this man would have stopped at nothing and would, indeed, still be harassing me to this day. It scares me to think what my life might be like if I hadn't taken a legal stand. It was the best thing I ever did!

Dear Jamie:

You have much to be proud of and I hope you know that! You went the extra mile...took those much-needed additional steps to ensure that he couldn't, under any circumstance, interfere in your life. I can only imagine how sad and terribly difficult it must have been for you but you did it and I am proud as hell because you are one of the survivors!

Indeed, **Phase Two** of the suffering can be dangerous to our recovery only because it's a hard concept to understand. If we don't understand it, we can easily succumb to feelings like anxiety and depression and in many cases, we even go back. For this reason, if, right now, you are feeling the compulsion to make contact even though you've accepted the reality, it is imperative that you pay attention to what I'm trying to tell you. Listen up...you are NOT crazy! There's a very good psychological reason why you feel crippled with sadness *even knowing what you know about narcissism and despite the fact that you don't even want him back*. The feeling of having to let go – to be free of the madness – is often difficult to appreciate.

Initially, we miss the delusions simply because, as maddening as they were, they kept us entertained and busy. The atmosphere around a narc is rarely boring and being caught up in the drama and the chaos...well, we hate it and love it at the same time. Therefore, we may feel bored, confused at our own confusion. Depression is not uncommon as the narcissistic noise subsides and we come to our senses. This is the first phase of finding sanity and you must embrace it. In other words, be glad that you're sad, my friends. You are moving successfully through the pain. Giving up easily is our biggest mistake and we do it over and over even though we know it's wrong. For the first time in forever, allow yourself to feel the pain and then move forward. Believe it or not, this is not a life or death situation. Follow the path that leads in the opposite direction - away from the suffering - and have faith that whatever you are feeling shall pass (and quickly).

One night, towards the very end of my "relationship", I found myself once again stuck in the rabbit hole at the beginning of an unexpected discard. My narc had, once again, caught me off guard and disappeared. At first, I was simply wrapped in denial, being stupid. Here it was, the second or third day of his silence and I was still conjuring up excuses, refusing to believe that I'd been deliberately duped again. But as the day went on and my calls went straight to voice mail, the weight of familiar doom started coming on down. I made one more attempt to call….and then it was done. He had skedaddled off the grid again, that *rat fucking bastard.*

As the realization sunk in, I prepared myself for the typical transformation. I knew that in about five seconds, whether I liked it or not, I was going to shrink in both size and spirit right in my office chair. Seriously, this moment would, over the years, become very defining. Tears would well up, my stomach would spasm, my lips would start quivering…and then BANG, all my sanity would spontaneously combust. Then, I simply waited for the tears so I could suffer center stage in my shit show like some Blair Witch rendition of Alice in Wonderland. It was always *that* bad. But that night, something in the script changed and I got control of myself. I actually thought about what I was about to do and all the suffering and I decided not to go there. In my book *When Love Is a Lie,* I describe a similar game-changing moment where I quit my decade long "desperation ritual" of driving across town at 3AM to leave notes on my narc's door during silent treatments. I got up to leave and suddenly what I was doing made no sense. In fact, I knew in that moment that it would cause me far more anxiety to go than to stay. And I never did it again.

This night, as I waited to crumble, I had an epiphany once again. Truthfully, it wasn't that complicated. There was simply no way I could go down again. I had too much to do and I wasn't ready for the pain. I imagined the typical weeks and months to come and said "no way". How I would get through it?...well, I knew this much: no matter what I did, **my suffering never changed anything.** The fact that I suffered or didn't suffer made no difference to the narc because he wasn't around to see it. This being true, why suffer? So, I made a conscious choice not to and this became life line until the not-so-bitter end.

Suffering is a process and you will need to move through it while moving away from it. You can do it. Same as you moved through phase one, so shall you move through phase two. Know in your heart that *our suffering changes not a single thing.* It doesn't change the big world, our world, the narcissist's world, the past, the future...not a thing. We can curl up in the fetal position, lose ten pounds, and even feel suicidal and the universe and everything in it just keeps moving. As I said, the final phase – the final "let go" before our mental freedom – is a detachment from the suffering. It is the last thing to go...the last remnant of the relationship. It feels very bittersweet but so what! You are almost there!

I remember staring out the window at the very end, about three months in, thinking, "Wow, this is really it. It is really over this time." It was an odd feeling and I waited for the gush of tears but again, it never came. There were no tears because there was no need. The feeling was awkward but I gave in to it. I allowed myself to think "wow, this is really, really OVER" without falling to pieces. I hadn't gone looking for him and had no desire whatsoever to do so. I knew that if he came to the door with that familiar knock, I wasn't going to answer. I had had enough and my heart…the Universe…knew it because there were no tears. I didn't feel like jumping for joy but I knew I didn't feel like dying either. I'll admit, crossing this threshold after 13-years of making *suffering about my ex* my reason for living was a very odd sensation. So, as I sat at the window looking out, I knew that, even as I struggled with acceptance, the truth was that this chapter of my life was over and all that suffering…well, it hadn't changed a thing.

Think about it…if we can come to realize and accept that all the love in our hearts can't change the narc, then we can certainly realize that our *suffering changes nothing* and choose to let it go. When you let it go, all the drama goes with it and it just doesn't get better than that.

Chapter XV:
The Truth About Forgiveness

Many people that I counsel entertain a notion that is widely popular in self-help circles and it is this: that to fully heal and recover from a break-up with the narcissist, we will first have to forgive this person. After all, the narcissist suffers…he or she just doesn't know it, right? *Wait - What!* Of course, I nip this notion in the bud during each phone call, ultimately lifting a burden and changing a few minds in the process. This idea about having to forgive your abuser before you can move on is, in my opinion, a bunch of bullshit.

The core of my forgiveness theory is this: *we don't have to forgive a narcissist for the pain he has caused us. We don't have to feel compassion about the fact that he unfortunately can't feel love. We don't have to be sympathetic and understanding about the bad childhood that he can't seem to get over. We don't have to do any of this. All we need to do is move along. The pain takes care of itself in recovery.*

Forgiving our abuser need not be our first order of business. As time passes, another feeling takes over that is akin to forgiveness but without the emotion. It is a natural detachment from the abuse that takes little effort. Forgiving a narcissist is very difficult and psychologists who say to focus on this *first* are doing a disservice to clients.

There was story in the news recently where a father was in court giving an impact statement prior to a judge's sentencing of the killer of his young daughter. This psychopath had killed 4 girls in the most brutal of ways and had been found guilty and, as is the norm, parents and family of the victims are given time to stand before the killer and the judge and say whatever is on their mind. It's always a sad scene that is hard to watch. Well, the dad of one of the victims is standing at a podium facing the judge with the killer seated directly behind him at the lawyers table. As the dad begins to speak, he turns to face his daughter's killer and the monster *grins at him*...an evil "I-don't give-a fuck" grin for all the TV world to see. The dad literally leaps up and dives head first over the table grabbing at the prisoner. The killer, who is handcuffed, jumps up and out of the way, still smiling, and everyone freaks out. The cops, of course, bear down on this poor father who is screaming and crying. He saw that grin and wanted to destroy it – and rightly so. They remove this dad from the courtroom AND the courthouse and he never gets to say anything. Should this killer be forgiven? Will forgiving this killer make it easier for this heartbroken father to move on? I'm sure this psychopath had a horrible childhood and a narcissistic mother or father. Should we care? Does any of that *really* matter when the person who committed the atrocity is so clearly unfixable?

So, swap the psychopath with your narcissist. Sure, your narc may not have physically committed murder but this is only a technicality. He or she surely destroyed your sanity, squashing your self-esteem and making you doubt yourself and what you knew to be true. Your expectations were managed down so low that he or she COULD get away with "murder"...the murder of your sanity. Your narc may have disappeared without a word sometimes, leaving you in limbo, riddled with anxiety, and unable to move forward until the next reset. And the reset always came because this is the pattern of abuse that you allowed. He knew that you would ask no questions for fear he would leave again. He made you feel insignificant and then called you insecure. He created chaos day to day and accused you of being dramatic. When he was nice, he was very nice but you could never quite relax and he liked that. The sex may have been great but later you discovered that he practiced a lot outside of the relationship. He controlled all communications, using his cell phone as a Mission Control to juggle his secrets. Now, despite everything he's done, you still grieve. You accept that recovery is a long process and you sadly hunker down. Meanwhile, the narcissist continues on without skipping a beat. He doesn't care about your history together. He never did. Does it make sense that your first order of business in recovery is to forgive this person? Of course, it doesn't, but people really struggle with this.

The truth is that someone who makes a bad mistake but has total remorse and a narcissist who abuses freely with a

clear conscience should *not* be forgiven equally. One deserves forgiveness and the other deserves not a single thing. If you say to the mistake-maker, "You are a good person and we all make mistakes. I realize that you are sorry and I'm going to forgive you", the mistake-maker will likely cry tears of appreciation. If you say this to a narcissist, he will smirk, knowing that he got away with it. If you say this in front of a *room* of narcissists, they would likely burst into wicked laughter. Narcissists are the epitome of repeat offenders. Why waste perfectly good forgiveness?

We don't need to become martyrs to heal. We're not obligated morally or spiritually to forgive all the bad people in our lives for the pain they have caused. No matter what he or she tells you, your narcissistic ex has had a joyous wild ride at your expense for however long it took. The truth is that you've already gone the forgiveness route hundreds of times over the months or years and it served no purpose. *However, credit is due where forgiveness has already been shown, my friend.* It's time to credit yourself accordingly and move along.

From: Misadventure
I have been conflicted about whether I believe narcissists know right from wrong. My husband has several narcissistic traits but truly he does not experience "remorse" and I honestly believe now that he does not have a concept of when his actions have been hurtful or wrong. He does not understand "guilt" or "remorse" as we have

discussed this. He has attributed this to a difference between our religious backgrounds. He comes from a Christian background (that believes in forgiveness instead of guilt/remorse/punishment), versus my Jewish Old Testament indoctrination into clear cut rights/wrongs/ morality/remorse/guilt/punishment. I feel it's utter bullshit. If my husband has ever acknowledged his behaviors were wrong, it was mostly to appease me after a fight and me being hurt, and not to lose my love and support. BTW his transgressions never had to do with cheating, at least as far as I've been aware. The lies have been about money, mismanagement of finances, hiding his business endeavors from me, generally being secretive and making couple decisions or those regarding our children, without consulting me. Postscript: I never realized he was a narcissist until discovering it in another person I was close to. For a long time I attributed his secrecy, failure to take responsibility, his rages and finger pointing to having unmanaged ADD.

From: Me

Hi Misadventure,

I agree with you that his false-Christianity excuse is utter bullshit. When I say that "narcissists know right from wrong, they just don't give a shit", your husband would fall under that category. Narcissist are known for giving LUDICROUS excuses for their behaviors. He is no Christian, sister! He is using his "background" as an excuse to get away with reckless behaviors and he knows exactly what he is doing. Trying to brain-wash you into thinking that you are just like him is called PROJECTION and narcissists do it all the time. They project their inappropriate way of thinking onto you. Do not be deceived into thinking his way. You DO understand remorse and guilt, EVERYONE understands it, even a narcissist. The difference is that a narcissist could care less about reckless behavior and what it does to others. He will never say this or admit to thinking this way (because he knows it's not appropriate), but he knows right from wrong and he could care less. I have to admit, your husband has created a clever brainwashing technique and it obviously is working but only to a point or you wouldn't have written in. Again, do NOT be deceived and stop making excuses for his horrible flaws. He doesn't have un-managed ADD! He is a narcissist who is conveniently taking advantage of your forgiving nature. I agree that it is utter bullshit!

From: Julia

My ex narcissist husband knows what "society" says is right and wrong and will act accordingly when the situation calls for it. Or, in other words, he'll do what's "right" if it benefits him in some way to do so. I don't, however, believe that he personally agrees with what most of us would say is the right thing to do. His moral compass is turned around. It points towards him. Only HE determines what's right in his world. Therefore, I believe narcissists know exactly what they are doing. It's a choice. Especially if they are super intelligent like mine is (summa cum laude.) I believe they are always planning. The Puppet Master at work. It's all acting to them. Deciding what role to play, lover or torturer. Seriously, what consequences do they actually experience? Those of us who give them narcissistic supply are usually so well trained to forgive and forget, that they never experience any negative consequences for their atrocious behavior.

From: Me

Hi Julia,

I don't believe that narcs personally agree with what most of us would say is the right thing to do either. However, they do know what those "right" things are and will - reluctantly and periodically - concede in order to meet the status quo if it is beneficial. As for negative consequences, they do occur but because a narc feels no attachment to anything, they simply shrug their shoulders and move along as if it was no big deal (because, of course, it wasn't). The PAIN of the HIS consequence is subsequently felt by everyone else. Does that make sense? It's so twisted and convoluted, it's hard to describe. Thanks for sharing, girl!

From: Jenny

I totally agree. Everyone else feels the pain and consequences of their behavior. My ex lost a job once, but he actually knew he would if he continued with his actions. He did it anyway because he enjoyed what he was doing (sleeping around with employees) more than he cared about his job!

From: Over and Out

I was so angry that I sent an email to his work detailing all of his evil ways. How foolish, right?? I'm sure it didn't phase him, and he continues to sleep with anyone he can seduce. So this horrible man is now on a trip to Africa, posting about all his humanitarian endeavors, and has all his friends gushing over his wonderfulness. That only thing to do is keep moving on and hope that someday, somehow, he gets what he deserves!

Whether we forgive or not, the narcissist will always repeat the performance. This type of behavior keeps us limping around, crippled by a broken heart. We bargain with logic, issuing the narc what I call The Jesus Pass (*Forgive them Father for they know not what they do!*). The truth is that they *do* know right from wrong...they simply don't care. As good people, we *want* to forgive...to treat others as we would like to be treated. But when we're dealing with a narcissist, all bets are off. And for those who feel that, as Christians, forgiveness is mandatory, I beg to differ. I personally don't feel that any of us have the spiritual credentials to forgive at this level. With all due respect, this forgiveness people speak of…when it involves narcissism…is simply not our job in this lifetime.

From: Mary

Hi Over and Out,

Reading about how your ex is involved in humanitarian endeavors reminds me of my ex. When I met my husband, he taught 5th graders and the kids ADORED him. He could do know wrong. So I thought he must be a really great guy. My mistake. My clue should have been that the other teachers didn't care for him. His excuse? He spent too much time with the kids, and no time socializing with the faculty. What I didn't know about was narcissistic supply. Being with a group of 30 kids all day who idealized and loved him was a HUGE source of narcissistic supply for my ex. Now, in retrospect, I can clearly see him feeding on their energy. This is what makes it all so confusing. Narc can appear like giving, philanthropic people in service of the greater good on the surface. But if you dig deeper, or become involved with them, you soon realize they are only doing the things they do for the love, recognition, appreciation that they receive from their adoring audience.

From: Sherry

To Over and Out,

Yes, a narc's alter-personality is the most difficult to comprehend.

My ex comes across as the most spiritual, humanitarian, caring and kind person you can imagine to everyone in his career and life. Only the women he has been involved with know the truth about who he is. It is mind boggling to see how they can just drop us and the next day be out having a blast with someone else, all the while claiming they are a "good person". Also, it is amazing how we can look past the initial warning signs and allow these people to suck us back in with their charm. I am currently reading Zari's book for the second time, and it's pretty much the only thing that helps. I just found her website for the first time. I feel crippled and broken by this loss. I actually thought he was the one, and I was so fooled. I realize now that everything he does is for the sake of gaining love and admiration from others. Ugh.

From: Christine

Oh, narcissists don't deserve any "Jesus pass" at all! If they didn't know right from wrong, how do they seduce victims during the idealization phase? They obviously know enough about human nature to tell us what we want to hear and get us "hooked". They also tend to intermingle "good" times with the bad ones. During the devaluation, they know when they've been bad and might cause us to leave–so then, they'll give us brief glimpses of the idealization phase to keep us hooked, until they're ready with our replacements and can discard us. Or look at how they put on the sweet act during their "hoovers" afterwards–again, because they know they treated us badly, so they need to pour that act on to get us to return. I swear the narcissist just sensed when he'd gone too far and that I wanted to leave. So then, he poured on the sweet act again to get me to stay longer. This is why I blocked him after leaving for good, to prevent myself from falling for that again. No one can pull off this type of manipulation without knowing right from wrong. So leave and don't look back. They DO know right from wrong. So they COULD treat you well...but they CHOOSE NOT TO! So people have NOTHING to feel guilty about for leaving them. They chose to treat you badly, so they brought the consequences on themselves with you leaving. Do as I both say AND do...leave, don't look back, then move on to a healthy relationship with someone who treats you like gold, as you deserve (or, if you want to stay single that's great too...but whether you move on to another relationship or not, just do NOT stay with the narcissist no matter what)

From: Over and Out

I totally agree. I had a book about narcissists and he asked to borrow it. I swear he reads and knows exactly what to do. I have always said that he is totally aware of what he is doing. It's a game. He even told a girl that he lies to manipulate and get what he wants. I have left the relationship but still watch his posts in FB. It's still hard for me to give that up even though it is painful to see all his activities and all the people that adore him. But you are correct...leave and don't look back.

Okay, Zari, you're the only self-helper that thinks we don't have to forgive. What do you want me to do – become a bitter person? Of course not. I'm saying that you don't have to do anything at all except move along. Focusing on forgiveness as a priority in recovery will keep you in the loop. Let this person go and the rest – the healing - will take care of itself with no forgiveness required. If you believe that forgiving the narcissist for abusing you is going to "prove" that he took nothing from you, you are very mistaken.

Oh, so you want me to be nasty and mean whenever I see him? Of course, not. I want you to go no contact and let him be. He doesn't deserve to see or hear from you in your lifetime. Eventually, while the feeling you get can't be described as "forgiveness", you *will* come to a place of peace and acceptance. And it won't even matter if he knows it. I don't hate my ex. He's here in town and, periodically, I will get a clue that he's alive and well. I don't wish him ill will...all that has really passed. What I feel now is nothing. Now, mind you, nothing and *numbness* are two different things. I remember feeling numb and as long as I "felt" numb, I was still in pain. Feeling numb is like being in shock. I understand that now and it didn't feel good. On the other hand, feeling nothing feels pretty great. And I did it all without having to "forgive" a thing!

So, how is it, then, that I feel like I've forgiven other ex's and it worked out great? Break-ups that occur in even the most dysfunctional of normal relationships are different. In those relationships, even with a broken heart, we don't typically think about going "no contact". We just know we have to *go* and the other person will do the same. Why? Because it's *over* and that's what two "normal" people do when they break-up....they actually *do* go their separate ways. As time passes, healing all wounds, we're simply not going to hate this person or wish any ill will. Some of us have even reconnected with certain exes and remain friends. How can this happen? Do we forgive this person for the pain that he or she may have caused us? Sure we do, but the truth is that we *healed* and the forgiveness happened naturally.

Relationships with narcissists are different. The break-up is not normal. Think about it... in order to be close to this person, our *entire existence became about forgiving.* Forgiving was *what we did.* We forgave behaviors, cheating, and indifference. Forgive, forgive, and forgive again. And what good did it do? The narcissist simply took advantage. Once we go no contact, we're DONE with the forgiving. Unlike what can happen after a "normal" break-up with a "normal" partner, there will *not* come a time, once you've recovered, when you feel like "being buddies" with a narcissistic ex. Forgiveness, by definition, will *not* happen naturally because it's *not supposed to.* Instead, as time passes, you will come to a place of total detachment where you feel nothing and it will feel great. In these types of break-ups, forgiveness, by definition, has nothing at all to do with how you heal. You are going to heal on your own simply by moving along and forgiving yourself…and the rest will take care of itself. Have confidence in what you know to be true and you *will* do the right thing.

Chapter XVI:
Vacancy In the Rabbit Hole

When my readers express an inability to get on with life, I understand this completely. I spent many a day curled up in the fetal position, unable to get up for the simplest of daily chores and activities. I couldn't get out of the rabbit hole. Sometimes I would sob and sob until the sound of my crying reverberated throughout the apartment. Although we realize that NC has to happen for us to "get better", it's knowing how to push through the unbelievable sadness that escapes us. Our friends and family become sick and tired of hearing about it but we feel compelled to speak of nothing else. I understand that this is a very hopeless feeling and so I developed a little game to get me through it called **Postpone & Pretend.**

You see, like you, I knew that, even amidst all my sadness, life had to go on. We have families and friends and we also have *jobs* that we depend upon for sheer survival. When we feel this bad, we can easily mess this up. Do not allow this to happen. The truth is that your sadness about the separation only exists within a very small part of your reality that only you see and feel. In the larger, more important part of your world, nobody really cares that you miss this monster and it's only because you mention it that they even know. One day I suddenly realized that if I walked around *pretending* everything was cool in my world, no one on the outside would be the wiser. Everyone would *believe* that all was good.. It occurred to me that I had the power to do this…to change how I *appeared* to the outside world while this "no- contact" pain was happening. In other words, I could keep the sadness and anxiety a secret and just pretend.

The next time you are consumed with NC separation anxiety, just imagine how satisfied the narcissist would feel to know that the punishment you're subjecting *him* to makes you far more miserable than he or she will ever be. In fact, it's a good bet that the narcissist is never miserable at all! So, you've simply got to get up and keep moving.

It's all about changing your perspective. Forcing myself to change my thought process to one that allowed me *to postpone my sadness* for at least 24 hours (to start) was a miracle cure. When we feel broken-hearted over a break-up, the last thing we want to accept is that we will never ever think about this person again. As we have learned, we *want* to suffer over our decision to go NC because it is our suffering that has always kept us connected. As long as we suffer, there is always that chance for future contact whether we initiate it or they do. **We get conditioned to the fact that the best moments of the relationship always - and only - occur after a hefty bout of suffering on our part.** And it all starts with the anticipation of what's to come...the knock at the door or the make-up sex or the sudden text hoover. Sometimes it is simply the thought of the *possibility* of any of that that does it. Whatever it is (and it's different for everyone), the combination of mental anguish and the actual event, if it does occur, is about as close to a mental orgasm as we're ever going to get and it feels fucking great. It all comes down to that 'arousal-jag' and that oxytocin. *Who would have thunk it?*

So, as we suffer through No Contact, it's perfectly okay to play head games with ourselves to get us up and out of the bed. Whatever it takes, do it. For me, it was a game of postpone and pretend. By giving myself permission to suffer *tomorrow*, I was somehow able to get up and do the things that I needed to do *today*.

You must remember that although it's been trained to be codependent to this nonsense, your brain isn't stupid and knows *exactly* what it should be doing and thinking. Therefore, it doesn't take long to retrain it back to normal. So, when the alarm clock goes off and you feel like dying, *push off the pain and get up.* This is the first step in the process. No matter how bad you feel, the world is going to remind you that you have other responsibilities and you better learn to deal with it. Only you have the power to turn it around.

Simply POSTPONE THE SADNESS **FOR 24-HOURS** and tend to your business. Then, the very next morning, when the world screams again, POSTPONE THE SADNESS FOR ANOTHER DAY and force yourself up. Keep doing this day after day after day. Rinse and repeat until it becomes second nature. It really works, my friend. I'm not saying you have to get out of bed and dance a jig. The first step is to simply *get out of bed*.

Now, once you're up, you're going to find yourself smack-dab in the middle of a world that could give two shits about you missing the narcissist. What do you do then? You begin the second step in the process and **start pretending**. Now that you're up and about and not shirking your responsibilities, you have to act, for the most part, as if everything is fine. You must pretend that this day is like any other. You must act "as if" you can live your life without obsessing about what the narc is doing. Those around you do not need to suffer because of your grave relationship error. In fact, no one needs to know anything. If you pretend that all is well, you are going to have a better day and that's a fact. You are NOT being inauthentic. In fact, you are finding your way *back* to your authentic life.

From: Maryanne:

Mine is absent right now, as he was this time last year, and as he was, he says, from the woman before me, a couple of years ago. I don't believe he's seeing someone else, though that could just be naivety. He lives with his elderly parents, and he has a lot of mental health problems. He isn't on social media and I have no way of checking up on him, even if that was a good idea.

And it's over, so why would I want to know if he'd been cheating on me? He used to accuse me of cheating on him, but he's clinically paranoid - thinks people are trying to poison him, etc.

A couple of times his mother said she didn't recognize my voice on the phone. Now, was that because other women were calling? Could be although I always saw her as the only other woman. He has never left home for long, and he's 50. Ah, who knows?

I suspect he will not want to "reward" me with his presence at Christmas and that is fine. Being with him those last few weeks was horrific. He was threatening violence to everyone he knew. He was angry and hostile and oh God I hated being with him. But now, all the lonely cravings are setting in, of course. I do sometimes wonder if he was seeing a man. He did have a few friendships with men who were much, much younger than he was - friendships that I thought were suspicious despite the fact that he was fairly homophobic. I should probably have an STD test. How depressing all of this is.

From: Me

I am responding to this post before your first one only because I read too many things in your message that apply to my own ex's behavior so I simply had to share immediately.

You wrote: **Mine is absent right now, as he was this time last year, and as he was, he says, from the woman before me, a** *couple of years ago. I don't believe he's seeing someone else, though that could just be naivety.* Mine disappeared every October - late January every year and I'd have to say that each time I relied on my belief that he probably wasn't cheating on me to get me through it until he came back. I was wrong and, more than likely so are you. There's a reason why he leaves every year. He's expected someplace else.

He lives with his elderly parents, and he has a lot of mental health problems. He isn't on social media and I have no way of checking up on him, even if that was a good idea. Most single male narcissists have a safe haven (a room and an address) at one or both of the parents' home where we think they're living when they're not with us. My ex, who is also 50, did the same thing for 13-years (minus a couple of times that he actually rented his own apartment which was always short-lived and even then he still used his parent's address). Thinking that this is where they live also provides us comfort. The truth, however, is that they have no home of their own but that doesn't mean they have no place to live or go. It's just as easy for them to camp out at another person's house as it is for them to camp at our house while still maintaining the parent's home as "where they live". Mine wasn't on social media either and it was hard to find ANYTHING on him ANYWHERE but he was out there and he cheated.

He used to accuse me of cheating on him, but he's clinically paranoid – thinks people are trying to poison him, etc. Trust me, a narcissist only accuses his partner of EXACTLY what he's up to at any given moment. My ex, too, accused me of cheating and - yup! - he even accused me of trying to poison him on a few occasions. AND he thought people were following him too (on and off). This is all a distraction strategy to keep you from focusing on what he's REALLY doing. Boyfriends who really believe their girlfriends are cheating do not leave them alone every year over the holidays. It's not logical. As for your guy being "clinically" paranoid, I don't buy that for a minute. Everything you describe is typical behavior of a narcissistic dude who is juggling a couple things, that's all. You might as well have been dating MY ex - sounds like the exact same guy.

And being with him those last few weeks was horrific. He was threatening violence to people, he was angry and hostile and oh God I hated being with him. But now all the lonely craving has set in, of course. Narcissists always ramp up the volume of chaos a couple/few weeks right before they disappear. Mine did it every single time and that's how I started to know that a silent treatment was on it's way!! And, yes, I had the same lonely craving and this is intentional as well. Narcs make a lot of noise so that the inevitable silence will be deafening and we will become so sad for missing them that when they return, we'll take them back with little if any repercussions. This is called managing down our expectations of the relationship so that we eventually accept just crumbs of attention - and it works every time. Or as long as we continue to allow it.

I do sometimes wonder if he was seeing a man. He did have a few friendships with men much, much younger than him, which I thought was odd, and he is fairly homophobic. *I had the same suspicions about my guy and I have no doubt that our intuitions are spot-on. The narcissists that engage in covert homosexual activity are the ones who put up the biggest fronts such as safe havens at mom's house, no social media (that you know of), creating mental distractions and accusatory nonsense, etc. And mine had a love/hate relationship with his mom which did, in fact, make her the "other woman" over all those years. And let me say this....I, too, could never really find hard evidence about girls. Although certainly there was one he admitted to years ago and a few mysterious phone numbers that I traced to females after that, there was no hard proof. SO WHY THEN DID I STILL GET THAT NAGGING FEELING? Could it have been the elusive number of young male friends that he would speak of in passing yet I never got to actually meet? Or was it the phone numbers that I found that I did call and a guy would answer? Or the fact that he was fairly homophobic and made sure to tell me the odd story here and there of how some guy made a pass at him and how mortified he was? Something about all that always left me with a feeling that he was telling another lie or telling me a story "on purpose" to throw me off track. There were other, more personal things over the years that left me thinking about this and I'm sure you have plenty of other those reasons yourself.*

I should probably have an STD test. *Yes, you should. My ex came* back after the holidays passed for about two days before he disappeared again. During those two days, it felt to me like he just came back for sex. It was very strange. Then, two weeks later, he leaves a voice mail from a pay phone number saying that he just found out he had an STD and that I must have given it to him. I was mortified. To confirm, the next day, I get a call from the local Health Department stating that he indeed had been treated for an STD and they were given my name as his previous partner and that they suggested I get checked as well. In my state, they won't treat you unless you give them a name of who you might have infected or who may have infected you. Freaking out and PISSED, I got myself checked not once but twice and I was NEGATIVE. Of course, I was relieved but then something slowly dawned on me: he had already KNOWN he had the STD when he returned for those two days. He had wanted to infect me so that he could BLAME me....but his plot backfired when, thankfully, it didn't happen. Well, a month later he returned again, BEGGING me to believe that he had no clue HOW it happened but that he heard that you can be BORN with it. My shocked silence was his pass to push the reset button. Here's my point: check yourself. Your intuition is always right, sister. Even if you can't prove it, you're STILL right.

On my website, you will see a zillion stories like your own. It's as if we have lived the same life with only slight variations. But your story and mine - pretty much identical. It just is what it is.

I promise you, friend, that if you pretend and postpone

enough times, you're going to begin to get better and fast! You're going to retrain your brain to get a grip. What this Game of Life is all about is living in the moment....in the here and now. You've got to do it. In the here and now...in this very moment, the N is going about his (or her) business, playing his or her Game of Life in typical narcissistic fashion, and they are going to do this whether you are suffering or not. Since your suffering changes nothing, you can make the choice to move along. What you're doing and how you're feeling doesn't make a bit of difference to this person at all. So, knowing this to be true (that he/she is going to do it no matter what!), which do you choose to do – sink or swim? Think about that. No Contact is the right decision.

You have every right to postpone (the suffering) and pretend (to be happy). The Universe will appreciate your efforts to get better and you will be richly rewarded. Eventually, you'll find yourself simply getting up and going forth. You'll discover that, by pretending to be okay, you can actually share a laugh with a friend without feeling as if you forgot something. The truth is that No Contact has to happen in order for you to live your life in the manner that you deserve. If it takes a few months of playing a game of postpone and pretend on your game board of life to make it happen, so be it. It worked for me and I know it can – and will – for you as well. It's going to be a challenge but I know you can do it. Have faith in yourself and go forth and be happy.

Final Thoughts

As I thought of ways to close this book, I put myself back in the shoes of a narcissist's partner. What did it take for me to finally "get it"? How did I escape the debilitating separation anxiety of silent treatments? What was it that finally convinced me to take action? I thought about it and then I knew…..*proof.* The answer, for me, was that it took proof. There had to be evidence that "no contact" would work before I went "all in" and meant it. Like most us, I had to have proof of a happy ending before I'd let myself believe. Well, I found that proof in the stories of survivors and for you, perhaps, it will be my story. Let me be your evidence that the break up is survivable. I promise you that it is *not* the end of the world. It is, in fact, a new beginning. Now, as a Narcissist Abuse Recovery (NAR) Coach, I speak with hundreds of people – many on a regular basis – and I see people make it to the finish line over and over. I'm not saying it's easy…but I'm telling you it will happen.

As I finish this book, I am a little over seven years out and life is fine. Without a doubt, it is *you* who has helped *me* to get better and to get on with my life. Because of my books and my blog, I have met and communicated with amazing and wonderful people. It has certainly been a privilege.

One of the truths about life is that it continues whether we like it or not. Yes, time really does heal all wounds *just like we've always been told.* But for time to do the healing, we have to allow it to do its work without resistance. We have to have faith in what we know to be true about this relationship situation. Sometimes, when things that are broken are proven unfixable, we have to let go and walk away. It's not always our job to pick up the pieces. We have to decide if we really want to live with this anxious feeling forever. The anxiety of being apart from this person is *not* far worse than the anxiety we feel when we're together...we only imagine that it is. Narcissists condition us to feel that way by creating our reality and then using it against us. If we don't choose to take our power back, the alternative is unthinkable. No Contact is your ticket to freedom. I'm here to tell you that the ride is survivable and you, my friend, are going to survive!

Here are four more tips to help you on your way!

1. **Decide TO STOP SUFFERING.** Why? Because our suffering changes nothing so we can actually choose which way to go. Repeat this over and over all day whenever you get that twinge. Understand that you suffering behind the scenes while the narc goes about his business is completely illogical and non-productive.
2. **Keep things in perspective.** Don't let your imagination run wild. In the narcissist's world, today is the same as yesterday. Nothing new under the sun. YOU are the only

one being affected by ANYTHING happening in the relationship, good or bad. The narcissists lives on a flat line with you and your world being the only blips on the screen. In your relationship, the biggest problem is that you've made yourself out to be far more important in the narc's world than you really are. To the narc, you are no more important than the person that came before you and anyone that will come after and they won't be any more important as you. THINK FLATLINE.

3. **Relieve yourself of the burden of explaining.** From here forward, if you haven't done it already, never explain a single thing about your relationship to anyone and this includes the narc! In the case of the narcissist, he or she KNOWS exactly what they've done and why you feel hurt or jealous or insecure or sad or whatever.

4. **Stop reacting and observe.** A narc LOVES it when, say, he accuses you of something ridiculous that he likely is already doing and you freak out, trying to explain to him why he's so wrong.

5. **Be happy because you deserve it. You are perfect just the way that you are.**

Suffering, while inevitable, is absolutely optional. As normal people, we will always feel compelled to "attach" to people, places, and things. However, this doesn't leave us powerless. Watch your intention and protect your boundaries and the rest will fall into place. Do not participate in a narcissist's Game of Life. Be honest and thoughtful and embrace your empathetic nature because, in these volatile times, it is needed more than ever. Let's work together and if we feel confused, there's always someone on the team who understands. We are, after all, in this together and recovery, I promise, is just around the corner and only a phone call away.

Speak With Zari

If you'd like to speak with me about what you're going through, please know that I offer <u>affordable phone consultations</u>. Together, we can change the outcome of your experience. Stay strong, my friends, and always know that I'm here to support you!

If you enjoyed this book, please do submit a review to Amazon! It would be most appreciated.

ABOUT THE AUTHOR

Zari Ballard is a home-based Freelance Writer/Author (and single mom!) who resides in sunny Tucson, Arizona at the base of the beautiful Catalina Mountains. In 2005, four years after her son's diagnosis with child-onset schizophrenia, Zari set aside the corporate rat race in lieu of a home-based career as a Freelance Writer. A leap of faith that could have gone either way, the choice was meant-to-be and she has never looked back.

Now, motivated by the success of her first book, *When Love Is a Lie*, Zari plans to ride the wave of self-publishing as far as it will take her. Alongside *When Love Is a Lie, Stop Spinning, Start Breathing, & Vacancy in the Rabbit Hole,* Zari has also published a book about female narcissism entitled *When Evil Is a Pretty Face*.

In addition, Zari now hosts the **'When Love Is a Lie' Video Blog Podcast on YouTube** where she discusses, mincing no words, all topics related to narcissism in relationships. Be sure and stay tuned!

Visit & Subscribe to [Zari's YouTube Channel](#)

Visit Zari's advice-filled blog [TheNarcissistPersonality.com](#)

If you enjoyed this book, please do submit a review to Amazon! It would be most appreciated.

Thank you for reading!

Made in the USA
Monee, IL
06 January 2022